Arthur Myers

On the Etiology and Prevalence of Diseases of the Heart Among Soldiers

Arthur Myers

On the Etiology and Prevalence of Diseases of the Heart Among Soldiers

ISBN/EAN: 9783337303457

Printed in Europe, USA, Canada, Australia, Japan

Cover: Foto ©ninafisch / pixelio.de

More available books at **www.hansebooks.com**

ON

THE ETIOLOGY AND PREVALENCE

OF

DISEASES OF THE HEART AMONG SOLDIERS.

THE "ALEXANDER" PRIZE ESSAY.

"TEMPORA MUTANTUR NOS ET MUTAMUR IN ILLIS."

BY

ARTHUR B. R. MYERS,
ASSISTANT-SURGEON, COLDSTREAM GUARDS.

LONDON:
JOHN CHURCHILL AND SONS, NEW BURLINGTON STREET.

MDCCCLXX.

By Permission.

TO

SIR GALBRAITH LOGAN, M.D., K.C.B.,

DIRECTOR-GENERAL ARMY MEDICAL DEPARTMENT; PRESIDENT OF THE
ALEXANDER MEMORIAL COMMITTEE,

This Essay is dedicated by the Author, in grateful acknowledgment of his kindness in granting the Author permission to attend the Course of Instruction given at the Army Medical School, Netley, during the past winter, thus enabling him to gain most valuable information on this subject, as well as on many others, without which this short Treatise could not, in the competition to which it has been submitted, have had applied to it the motto of his Regiment,

"NULLI SECUNDUS."

CONTENTS.

	PAGE
INTRODUCTORY REMARKS ...	1
PREVALENCE OF DISEASE OF THE HEART IN THE ARMY COMPARED WITH OTHER CLASSES...	2
THE FORMS OF DISEASE OF THE HEART SO PREVALENT IN THE ARMY ...	20
CAUSES OF HEART DISEASE, ETC. ...	22
GENERAL SUMMARY ..	81
MEASURES PROPOSED TO CHECK HEART DISEASE IN THE ARMY...	84
CONCLUDING REMARKS	92

AN ESSAY

ON THE

ETIOLOGY AND PREVALENCE OF DISEASES OF THE HEART AMONG SOLDIERS.

"Tempora mutantur nos et mutamur in illis."

THAT the above subject should have been the one chosen by the executive committee of the "Alexander Memorial Fund" for the first competitive essay, is the strongest evidence of the importance they attach to it; and, as it is one which has for some time attracted my attention, I trust the following remarks will meet with their approval, and contribute to such an investigation of this class of diseases as may ultimately tend to lessen their general prevalence in the army. *Introductory remarks.*

In the first volume of the *Transactions of the Medical and Physical Society of Bombay* (1836), are published the views of the late Dr. Hunter, 2nd Queen's, on this subject; and in his annual report for 1839, Dr. Nicholson drew special attention to their prevalence among the troops *Earliest records of observations on heart disease in the Army. Hunter. Nicholson.*

in the Cape Colony; and these medical officers were the first, so far as I can learn, to record observations of this kind.

Of late years the subject has been so ably treated by Drs. Maclean, Parkes, Aitken and others (from whose writings I shall hereafter freely quote), that I feel my remarks can claim but little originality, and that I can but hope to strengthen their statements, and only here and there add a little new matter.

<small>Rare diseases of heart not to be dwelt upon.</small>
I take it for granted that in this essay on diseases of the heart *in the soldier*, it is not necessary to enter fully into all the very numerous diseases of this organ from which all classes of mankind are liable to suffer, provided that those chosen for special comment are shown to be the all-important representatives of their class.

I shall divide my subject into the four following parts:—

<small>Division of subject into four parts.</small>
I. Prevalence of diseases of the heart in the army compared with other classes.

II. Particular forms of disease so prevalent.

III. Causes of the same.

IV. Remedies proposed.

Comparative Prevalence.

<small>·I. Comparative prevalence.</small>
Accurately compiled statistics on a large scale must be considered valuable aids in strengthening the statements of authors, and

I shall, therefore, make free use of those published by the Army Medical Department, &c.; but for the following reasons it appears to me that no correct comparison can be made of the relative extent of heart disease in the army and civil population of this, and certainly far less of any other country.

1. Because there are many differences in the two classes, both in the diseases of the heart as well as in the causes to which they owe their origin. *Reasons why correct statistical comparisons cannot be made between army and civilians of any country with regard to this disease.*

2. Because on enlistment the soldier (it must be presumed) has a healthy heart, whereas, at the same age, diseases of the heart are by no means uncommon in the civil population, as shown by the large number of rejections of recruits for the same, and therefore, any comparison must be in the soldier's favour.

TABLE I.
Recruits.

Table I. Recruits rejected for heart disease.

Year.	Total Examined.	Rejected for Heart Disease.	Ratio per 1,000.
1864	27,754	549	19·78
1865	24,891	553	22·22
1866	20,410	513	25·13

3. Because by far the largest proportion of our soldiers affected with heart disease are invalided, and return to their homes, and

should they in course of time die from the same, their deaths, registered on the civil list, must unfairly increase the relative mortality in this class; whilst the army mortality is greatly lessened, and it is in the mortality only of the two classes that any analysis of the kind can be made.

Netley records of invaliding for heart disease.

The records of Netley Hospital illustrate this fact well; thus, between March 10, 1863, and March 10, 1869, 1,635 invalids were admitted from foreign stations suffering from heart disease. Of these, 24 died at Netley, 1,322 were discharged the service, 276 returned to their duty, and 13 remained under treatment.

4. Because, owing to this invaliding and to many taking their discharge at or before the expiration of their first period of service, a considerable majority of those serving are under thirty years of age; whereas mortality from disease of the heart in the civil population greatly increases with advancing years, and therefore, no very definite results can be obtained by comparing the army with civilians in other than short periods of life, and army statistics of this disease in quinquennial or decennial periods are not, I believe, drawn up.

The following comparison between the army at home for seven years and the civil male population of London in 1861 (the year of the last census), gives a fair estimate of the relative extent of deaths from all causes in the two classes at different ages, as well as the mortality from diseases of the heart.

Comparisons of deaths from all causes in army and civil population, also from diseases of the heart.

I have chosen the period twenty to forty-five for the civil population, as civilians of an age between fifteen to twenty cannot compare with "soldiers under twenty," and as, according to the statistics, there are but few soldiers serving after the age of forty-five.

Reason for limiting age period to 20 to 45.

TABLE II.

Statistics of Deaths from all causes of Army and Civil Population within Periods of Age, as given; also of Deaths from Diseases of the Heart, &c., but in a more condensed form so far as the Army is concerned.

Age.	Strength.	Deaths from all Causes.	Ratio per 1,000.	Deaths from Diseases of Circulating System.	Ratio per 1,000.
ARMY :					
20 to 24	131,452	754	5·73		
25 to 34	137,971	1,275	9·24		
35 to 45	27,690	457	16·5		
Total ...	297,113	2,486	8·36		
CIVILIANS :					
20 to 24	122,548	885	7·22	29	·23
25 to 34	214,423	2,075	9·67	128	·59
35 to 45	170,434	2,624	15·39	236	1·38
Total ...	507,405	5,584	11·	393	·77
Army, *vide* Table III...	285,969			259	·9

The civil statistics refer to the males of London.

Comments on Table No. II.

It will thus be seen that though the death-rate in the army is much lower than in the civil male population in the first period, it is nearly equal in the second, and higher in the third; and that, notwithstanding the above-mentioned causes tending to diminish greatly the army ratio of deaths from diseases of the heart, it is still in excess of the civil ratio. A little allowance must, however, be made for the omission of civilians corresponding to "soldiers under twenty," but the strength and deaths of soldiers in this period are too limited to be of importance.

Why statistics include diseases of circulatory system en masse.

These statistics refer to diseases of the circulatory system *en masse*, for, with the exception of aneurism, the deaths from this order of Class III. of the late nomenclature, are almost entirely attributable to one or other diseases of the heart, and also because in the Registrar-General's return the order is divided only into Pericarditis, Aneurism, and *Heart Disease, &c.*

Inspector-General Lawson's statistics, &c.

Inspector-General Lawson gives the following statistics of death from these diseases, *vide* Army Medical Report for 1866:—

Period 1859 to 1865 inclusive.
Age 15 to 44. Civil Population ... ... ·48 per 1,000
  „   Army ... . ·84 „

Excluding aneurism, however, he more nearly approximates them:—

Civil Population ... ... ·45 per 1,000
Army ... ... ·50 „

And he remarks that, were the soldiers discharged from the service on account of heart disease, retained until their cases terminated fatally, as in civil life, the ratio of mortality would be considerably higher.

In 1864, a Committee, appointed by the Government to investigate the subject of heart disease in the army, arrived at the conclusion that the relative proportion of heart cases decreased with age, thus— *Statistics and remarks of a committee appointed by Government to investigate the subject of heart disease in the army.*

Heart cases to total invalids
{ Under 20 ... 1 in 5·45
20 to 24... ... 1 in 6·44
25 & upwards ... 1 in 8· }

The ratio per 1,000 of invaliding being—

1861 to 1863 inclusive
{ Under 20 ... 2·19 per 1,000
20 to 24 ... 4·57 „
25 & up. ... 5·02 „ }

showing an apparent increase with age, which necessitated a comparison with the invaliding from all causes—

Invaliding from all causes
{ Under 20 ... 11·93 per 1,000
20 to 24 ... 29·45 „
25 & up. ... 39·4 „ }

And then, comparing the advance from 29·45 to 39·4 with that from 4·57 to 5·02, they calculated that if the two had been equal, the invaliding over twenty-five years of age would have been for heart disease 6·1 instead of 5·02;

and from these and other comparative analyses they decided that there was an excess of heart cases among young soldiers.

The following is a more general abstract from their statistical tables:—

	Age.	Died of Heart Disease.	Invalided for Heart Disease.	Deaths from all causes.	Invalided for all causes.
1861 to 1863	Under 20	……	2·19	2·03	11·93
	20 to 24	·12	4·57	5·65	29·45
	25 & up.	1·56	5·02	10·66	39·40

And now, if I compare the deaths from disease of the heart in this table with those of civilians in my own, I find as follows:—

Age.	Army.	Civilians.
20 to 24 …	·12	·25
25 and up.	1·56	·94

And thus it would appear that though the death-rate in the army from this disease is less than in the civil population in the first, it is greater in the second period.

Statistics of army and navy specially good for comparison.

I shall now proceed to compare the army with the navy, and it is specially through the agency of this service that the extent of heart disease in the army can, I think, be most fairly estimated, as the tendencies to error, to which I have above referred in connection with the civil population, do not here exist.

The navy, it might naturally be assumed, would show a greater death-rate from this cause than the army, owing to the abnormal strains frequently imposed on the sailor's heart by the extreme and sudden violent exertions which are incidental to his work. *Why navy should be liable to suffer from heart disease.*

I was recently informed by an Inspector-General of the Navy that he had often observed intense excitement of the heart's action produced in young sailors by running aloft, manning the yards, &c., and that he had at times almost felt surprise at not having seen this end fatally. He added that many men were invalided for functional disease of the heart attributable, in his opinion, to the above.

Connected in a measure with this point are the following remarks of Dr. Peacock (*vide* "Lectures on Valvular Disease of the Heart," p. 65), with reference to the great extent of heart disease among the men who work in the tin and copper mines of Cornwall, and who have to return to the surface by ladders, there being but few mines in which any mechanical means are provided for bringing them up. "In this way," he writes, "an hour or more is spent by the men in climbing, and when they reach the surface they are usually much out of breath and their hearts beat violently." . . . . . *Heart disease of Cornish miners (Peacock).*

"The cardiac effect I conceive chiefly to arise from the distention and over-action of the heart in the prolonged exertion of climbing."

The following statistics, however, clearly prove that the navy loses much fewer men from disease of the heart, &c., than the army :—

TABLE III.

Diseases of the circulatory system in the Foot Guards and Infantry in the United Kingdom compared with the Navy during the period 1860 to 1865 inclusive.

ARMY.	Strength.	Admitted.	Died.	Ratio per 1,000.	Invalided.	Ratio per 1,000.
1860	55,079	451	71	1·28	215	3·9
1861	54,500	624	39	·71	375	6·88
1862	49,332	483	31	·62	251	5·08
1863	44,291	440	45	1·01	208	4·69
1864	40,539	345	36	·88	213	5·25
1865	42,228	391	37	·87	244	5·75
Total	285,969	2,734	259	·9	1,506	5·26
NAVY.						
1860	64,025	493	44	·68	186	2·9
1861	62,485	594	39	·62	248	3·96
1862	58,870	561	41	·69	207	3·53
1863	54,090	532	29	·53	196	3·62
1864	53,000	567	46	·86	182	3·43
1865	51,210	507	29	·56	165	3·22
Total	343,680	3,254	228	·66	1,184	3·44

Army suffers more than navy.

These statistics are not carried back beyond 1860, as in 1859 certain changes were made in the army returns which prevented the diseases being specified for which invalids of regiments serving at home were discharged the service; but, though in a measure limited, they are amply sufficient to show that the army loses a far larger proportion of men than the navy from the diseases under consideration.

Liability to error in comparing navy with army statistics.

The naval statistics do not quite coincide with those published in the annual official returns, as I have deducted "hæmorrhoids" from the diseases which are included in the circulatory system in this service, this disease in the army returns being entered in the digestive system in accordance with the nomenclature.

I have again referred to the subdivision of Class III., under consideration, *en masse*, in consequence of "functional and organic disease of the heart" in the naval returns having too wide a signification to allow of a more minute analysis being satisfactorily made.

Statistics open to improvements.

It is, I think, to be regretted that a greater similarity has not been adopted in the statistical returns of the two services, and to be hoped that the new nomenclature will effect this, and also be the means of allowing observations to be made on the relative extent of aortic and mitral diseases, which the late nomenclature rendered impossible.

I shall now refer to the Metropolitan Police, Mr. Holmes, the Chief Surgeon, having kindly forwarded me his annual reports, and compare them with the Foot Guards.

Heart disease in army and police of London.

Foot Guards and Police in the United Kingdom.

	Strength.	Died from Heart Disease, &c.	Ratio per 1,000.	Invalided for Heart Disease, &c.	Ratio per 1,000.
Foot Guards. 1863 to 1866 inclusive...	19,516	15	·8	63	3·2
Police. 1867 to 1868 inclusive...	16,749	5	·29	23	1·37

It is only since 1866 that annual sick returns of the police force, such as those from which I have made the above abstract, have been published, and consequently a comparison between the two services must be limited, but the difference is too great to admit of any doubt of there not being some excess of the disease in the army; and I agree with Mr. Holmes, that the two services are well adapted for comparison in consequence of their being chiefly stationed in London.

The Government in 1867 having called for a return of the sickness and mortality among merchant seamen, I have been enabled to

Heart disease in merchant seamen.

obtain the following information, and thus to point out that there is a much smaller loss from heart disease, &c., in this service than in the army, but I have no doubt that these statistics are somewhat open to error.

Merchant Seamen.

Year.	Strength.	Deaths from Heart Disease, &c.	Ratio per 1,000.
1866	196,371	70	·35

<small>A just estimate of heart disease in various armies cannot be formed by statistics.</small>

It appears to me impossible to form a just estimate by statistics of the relative extent of diseases of the heart in the various armies of Europe, for many reasons, of which the most important is the great difference in the length of service in the several Continental States, being in some very short; and the experience of the English army tending to the belief that, as a rule, prolonged military service is necessary for the full development of these complaints.

<small>Heart disease in French and Prussian armies (Parkes).</small>

Dr. Parkes, in his work on Hygiène, states that in the French army the deaths from heart disease are about one-third our loss, and that in the Prussian army Engel gives only ·31 deaths out of every 100 as owing to organic heart disease, pericarditis and aneurism not being included.

<small>Heart disease in Prussian army (Münnich).</small>

Dr. Münnich, of Berlin, from whom I have received much interesting information concerning the health of the Prussian army, has been unable to give me any accurate statistics on this point. Referring, however to one portion of the army, he writes:—

"In the guards stationed at Berlin and Potsdam from 1846 to 1862 0·74 per cent. died of organic heart disease, the deaths of the civil population of Berlin from the same cause and during the same time being 1·82 per cent.

"From this it would appear at first sight as if the army were much better off than the civil population in this respect, but the following must be taken into consideration:—

"1. That our soldiers are only recruited from young, healthy, strong men.

"2. That they are invalided on showing symptoms of heart complaint, and therefore seldom die as soldiers."

The statistics I have already given being, I think, sufficient to prove the much greater extent of heart disease in our army than in the other classes of men quoted, I will now place them in order, and then proceed to compare its relative frequency among the troops serving in various countries as given in the Army Medical Report for 1867.

TABLE IV.

The relative extent of Heart Disease, &c., in the Army, and various other bodies of men."

	Period.	Strength.	Deaths.	Ratio per 1,000.	Invalided.	Ratio per 1,000.
ARMY.—Footguards and Infantry	1860 to 1865	285,989	259	·9	1,506	5·26
Civil Male Population of London (20 to 45)	1861	507,405	393	·77	...	...
NAVY	1860 to 1865	343,680	228	·66	1,184	3·44
Merchant Seamen	1866	196,371	70	·35	...	...
Metropolitan Police	1867 to 1868	16,749	5	·29	23	1·37

TABLE V.

Ratio of Deaths in the Army at various Stations from Diseases of the Circulatory System, and from all causes.

1860 to 1866.	Circulatory System.	All causes.	1860 to 1866.	Circulatory System.	All causes.
United Kingdom	·95	9·33	Ceylon (Native troops, ·8)	1·12	24·53
Gibraltar	·74	10·71	Australia	2·21	16·93
Malta	·73	9·18	New Zealand	1·72	
Canada	1·19	35·58	China (Native troops, ·84)	1·24	57·75
Bermuda	1·12		Japan	1·74	
St. Helena	·48	10·57	India { Bombay, ·79; Bengal, ·96; Madras, 1·26 }	1·	27·48
Cape of Good Hope	1·90	18·44			
Mauritius	·55				

According to the last table, there certainly is a great variation in the ratios of death, both from heart disease and from all causes, but it is not nearly so great in the former as in the latter, if only those stations are taken into consideration where we have a great number of troops; and this is especially remarkable with regard to India, where the combined ratio of the three Presidencies is but little in excess of that of the troops in the United Kingdom, a fact to which I shall hereafter draw attention. *Great variation in death rate.* *Little difference in amount of death from heart disease in India and Great Britan.*

The statistics referring to countries in which we have but few troops are not on a sufficiently large scale to allow of any fair deductions being made from them, and I would therefore only draw special attention to the comparatively low death-rate from diseases of the circulatory system in Bermuda, China, and Japan; and, on the other hand, to the extremely high death-rate "from all causes" in these countries during the same period. viz., 1860 to 1866, inclusive. All these statistics, however, help to prove how much greater is the prevalence of diseases of the heart in the army than in the civil population; and, for the reasons I have already given, were I to add the invaliding to the death-rate in the army, I am confident that the combined total would prove a more accurate estimate of *Death from heart disease not great in certain countries where loss from all causes is very high.*

the real excess than by taking the deaths alone.

The following statistics show what little difference there is in the deaths from heart disease in the three chief divisions of the service in this country, and the slight excess in the invaliding for the same in the Infantry.

Heart disease in three arms of the service in Great Britain.

Diseases of circulatory system in three arms of the service in the United Kingdom, excluding Household Cavalry and depôts, 1860 to 1866, inclusive:—

	Strength.	Died.	Ratio per 1,000.	Invalided.	Ratio per 1,000.
Cavalry ...	62,117	50	·8	243	3·91
Artillery...	63,176	56	·88	223	3·52
Infantry...	168,385	144	·8	891	4·37

According to Dr. Bryden's tables (*vide Indian Medical Gazette*, May 1, 1869) the reverse holds good in India, thus—

Heart disease in three arms of the service in India (Bryden).

Heart Disease and Aneurism.

1865 to 1867 (3 years).	Ratio of deaths per 1,000.	Ratio of invaliding per 1,000.
Cavalry ...	... 2·06	4·9
Artillery ...	... ·86	4·33
Infantry ...	... ·9	2·63

Statistics of heart disease in India must, however, show great variation, according to circumstances, as was shown in a very able article on the subject published in the *Standard* of March 27, 1869, and from which the following is extracted:—"The highest ratio of mortality from diseases of the circulatory system in Bengal in 1866, viz., 3·46, occurred amongst the troops who are reported 'on the march;' and an almost identical result is shown by an examination of the Bombay army in 1866, for whilst the death-rate from diseases of the organs of circulation of the total force (12,077) was only ·66, that of the troops on the march was 3·38 per 1,000, a very striking fact."

<small>High rate of death from heart disease among troops "on the march" in India (*Standard*).</small>

Dr. Bryden's statistical table, however, clearly proves that in India the cavalry and artillery suffer more from these diseases than the infantry, and such is the invariable opinion of the many army medical officers who have kindly given me their personal experiences,— a fact to which I shall again refer.

In the same article in the *Standard*, is given an interesting table of the ratio per 1,000 of cases of admission to the sick list from tubercular disease or consumption on the one hand, and diseases of the heart and great vessels at fifteen important stations during the year 1866, and a comparison is made with the civil population, the result being as follows:—

<small>Relative extent of heart disease and consumption in army and civil population (*Standard*).</small>

1866.	Ratio of admissions for consumption.	Ratio of deaths for same.	Ratio of admissions for Heart Disease, &c.	Ratio of deaths for same.
Army	11·7	1·88	11·4	2·0
Civil Population	...	3·4	...	1·05

Showing, therefore, that whilst in the army

the diseases of the circulatory system seem to be about as common as tubercular diseases, and the fatality of the two the same; in the civil population the former are only between a third and fourth as frequent.

II. The diseases of the heart prevalent in the army.

I shall now proceed to the next part of my subject,—viz., a consideration of the particular forms of disease of the heart and circulatory system found to prevail in the army.

On this point statistics will only give an approximate result, owing to the defective system of nomenclature; but the following table, which I have drawn up with the aid of the Army Medical Report for 1867, gives a general estimate of the relative extent of the special diseases therein enumerated.

TABLE VI.

The relative extent of Deaths and Invaliding in the Home Services owing to the various diseases of the Circulatory System in their order of frequency during the five years 1863 to 1867.

Diseases of the Circulatory System.	Deaths.	Ratio per 1,000 of total deaths.
Aneurism	138	431·23
Morbus V. Cordis	103	321·87
Hypertrophia Cord.	21	65·62
Degeneratio Cord.	21	65·62
Pericarditis	21	65·62
Morbus Cordis	5	15·62
Carditis	4	12·5
Atrophia Cordis	3	9·37
Atheroma Arteriosum	2	6·25
Varix	1	3·12
Syncope	1	3·12
Total	320	...

Diseases of the Circulatory System.	Invalided.	Ratio per 1,000 of total invalided.
Morbus V. Cord.	518	369·98
Varix	473	357·41
Hypertrophia Cord.	201	149·26
Morbus Cord.	37	27·48
Aneurism	35	26·
Carditis	29	21·54
Palpitatio	21	15·6
Pericarditis	17	12·63
Angina Pectoris	6	4·45
Atrophia Cordis	4	2·97
Syncope	3	2·22
Degeneratio Cord.	2	1·48
Total	1,346	...

By this table it will be seen that diseases of the heart and aneurism are almost entirely accountable for the deaths in this class, as I have already stated, the latter heading the list, and with morbus valvularum cordis comprising three-fourths of the total number. Pericarditis, on the other hand, gives only the same ratio as hypertrophia cordis, a disease which, in civil life, very rarely terminates fatally without other known lesion.

Disease of the heart and aneurism cause nearly all the deaths returned under "circulatory system."

In the invaliding table aneurisms take a low place, owing probably to the fact of difficulty of diagnosis causing many of them to remain unobserved during the lifetime of the sufferers, or until the disease has advanced too far to admit of the man being invalided. Combining, then, the deaths and invaliding as here given, the diseases of the circulatory system, excluding varix, which cause the great loss to the Army, are—

<small>The three most prevalent diseases of circulatory system, excluding varix.</small>

    1. Morbus Valvularum Cordis.
    2. Hypertrophia Cordis.
    3. Aneurism.

And, therefore, in passing now to the next part of my subject, it will be to these diseases my remarks will be more especially confined.

<small>"Carditis" and "Morbus Cordis" doubtful terms.</small>

As to the probably doubtful nature of the diseases included under "Carditis" and "Morbus Cordis," it is not necessary for me, I think, to make more than a passing comment.

Causes of Heart Disease in the Army.

<small>III. Causes of heart disease.</small>

<small>Heart's action easily disturbed.</small>

<small>Opinions of Corvisart.</small>

When we reflect upon the delicate, though simple mechanism of the heart, upon the instantaneous effects on its action by excessive mental as well as bodily excitement, it may well surprise us to observe how little its all-important functions are studied by us in every-day life. Corvisart (*vide* "Treatise on the Diseases of the Heart," p. 355, tr. Hebb) thus wrote of it:—" From the *punctum saliens*, noticed by Harvey, in the unformed rudiments of the embryo to the *ultimum mariens*, or the impotent palpitations of the right auricle of a man who has reached the latest period of life, this organ is incessantly in motion, pulsating milliards of times. Under this view alone, ought we not to be astonished that it is not more frequently diseased than it is? Do the different circumstances and actions of our life tend to moderate its movements? Far from it. The act of parturition, the squalling of infancy, laughing, crying, singing, the use of some instruments, dancing, running, wrestling, exertion and attitudes of every kind, modes of dress, the use and abuse of a thousand aliments and liquors, viruses, all the arts and trades necessary to the existence or pleasures of social life, and that ever-renewing and numerous crowd of moral affections for ever operating; all conspire against the freedom and regularity of the preserving and vital action of the heart."

Fortunately, however, for mankind, owing to its protected position and to its marvellous power of overcoming, within certain limits, the momentary or prolonged strains to which it is subjected, even by an increased development of its structure, if necessary, like an ordinary muscle, its efficiency is not materially diminished in men of healthy constitutions earlier than that of less important organs. *Heart is well protected, and can bear great momentary strains without injury.*

Now, the primary diseases from which the heart suffers in civil life are very few during that period of life which corresponds with the

From 20 to 45 disease of heart in civil life chiefly due to rheumatism and disease of kidneys, but not so in the army.

service of the soldier, and the two great sources of its affection in civil life—viz., rheumatism and disease of the kidneys, to which may be added gout, are those which are not equally common in the army.

Netley statistics and remarks thereon (Maclean)

In 151 cases of heart disease, taken from the clinical records of Netley Hospital (*vide* " Army Medical Report, 1867 "), Dr. Maclean found that in six only had the patients suffered from acute rheumatism. He points this out as a notable fact, and as a very sufficient answer to some who, without having been at the pains to inquire, or, indeed, without the means of doing so, have endeavoured to discredit those who, for some time past, have been inviting attention to the true cause of the suffering and loss from heart disease in the army.

Statement of Parkes.

Dr. Parkes (*vide* "Manual of Hygiène") states, " The two most common causes of heart disease in the civil population are rheumatic fever in the young and renal disease in older persons. The latter cause is certainly not acting in the army, and the former appears quite insufficient to account for the facts."

Disease of heart produced by renal disease (Bright)

That much of the heart disease in the civil population is caused by renal disease there can be no doubt, and in Vol. I. " Guy's Hospital Reports," Dr. Bright published a series of 100 cases of renal disease, in fifty-two of which there was hypertrophy of the heart; of these there were thirty-four free from valve disease, but eleven had disease in the coats of the vessels, leaving twenty-three without any probable organic cause for the marked hypertrophy of the left ventricle. The valves chiefly affected were the aortic and mitral. He attributed this amount of heart hypertrophy either to the altered quality of the blood affording irregular and unwonted stimulus to the organ immediately, or affecting so much the minute and capillary circulation as to render greater action necessary to force the blood through the distant subdivisions of the vascular system. Again, Dr. Senhouse Kirkes, in an original communication to the *Medical Times and Gazette* (Vol. xxxii. p. 515), states—"That structural disease of the kidneys, of such nature as to interfere permanently or for long with their functions, has among its most frequent and prominent accompaniments an hypertrophied condition of the left ventricle, is a fact now almost generally admitted by pathologists. . . . . This hypertrophy is due to the heart requiring greater force to propel the blood forward, loaded with the retained principles of urinary excretion, and also to the direct influence on the circulation resulting from the impeded transit of the blood through the kidneys."

Considering, therefore, that the army has a

[margin: Senhouse Kirkes.]

Soldier's life not strictly laborious.

decided advantage over the civil population as regards rheumatism and renal disease, that the work of the soldier is by no means laborious—indeed, generally occupying him but a few hours per diem—it might naturally be supposed that he would not suffer much from heart disease; but, as by the writings of those men who have of late years closely studied the subject, as well as by statistics, there are ample proofs to the contrary, some very important agents, unconnected in a great measure with civil life, must be present to cause the marked excess which has been observed.

Causes of heart disease (Sir W. Jenner).

Sir William Jenner, in his address on medicine to the British Medical Association at Leeds this year (*vide British Medical Journal*, July 31st), after referring at some length to heart disease, stated: "We have attained to this practical conclusion—viz., that, regarded in a clinical point of view, structural changes in the valves of the heart are referable to one of three classes, imperfection in development, acute endocarditis, degenerative changes; and yet further advance of clinical knowledge has shown that non-fatal acute endocarditis is almost limited to acute rheumatism, and that degenerative changes, sufficient in degree to interfere with function, do not occur in the valves of the heart till middle life, and rarely till advancing middle life."

According to these views, also, the soldier should suffer less than the civilian, were there no special predisposing cause of heart disease in his mode of life. Accepting such to be the case in explanation of the excess, various causes have been suggested, all of which are acknowledged to play some part in the same, though the more prejudicial effect of one in particular may, in the opinion of some men, be still *sub judice*. Indeed, there are probably a few, even now, who ignore anything of the kind, and it was but recently that an eminent physician expressed his opinion freely in military circles to the effect that he did not believe the heart disease of the army need be attributed to any exceptional causes, but to precisely the same as in civil life, the chief of which were rheumatism and Bright's disease. In consequence of this, all the invalids in Netley Hospital suffering from heart disease were one day collected together, and Dr. Parkes, at the request of Dr. Maclean, examined them. Of the total number—seventy—he found only two or three had any previous history of disease, rheumatic, renal, syphilitic, or otherwise, to account for the disease then existing; and he therefore expressed his unqualified opinion that the great bulk of these cases could only be attributed to causes which did not pertain to the civil population.

Marginalia: Special causes of heart disease in army denied. Dr. Parkes's evidence to the contrary.

28   DISEASES OF THE HEART

*What special causes?
India, &c.*

What, then, are these special causes?

The climate of India, and of other countries of like nature, may be advanced by some as having a marked influence in this respect; but from statistics the other conclusion must be drawn, for during the seven years, 1860 to 1866 (*vide* Table V.), the ratio is only ·05 per 1,000 greater than in the United Kingdom; and if the five years, 1860 to 1864, be taken, it is then considerably less, the total ratio for this period being ·85 per 1,000 (*vide Army Medical Report for* 1865). The invaliding ratio of the army in India during the same period cannot be given, owing to some of the statistics for 1864 not being available (*vide* Blue-book, 1864); but as it is only 3·88 per 1,000 for the years 1865, 1866, 1867, one cannot suppose that heart disease is specially prevalent among the troops in that country.

Functional derangement of heart in India.

Functional disease of the heart, I am informed, is very prevalent in India, and it is in part attributed to the great heat; and in the Army Medical Report for 1860, page 23, it is stated that a number of men had been sent home labouring under affections of the heart, in many cases purely functional, the result of service in hot climates.

Sir Ranald Martin, in his work on Tropical Climates (p. 640, 2nd edition), writes:—" I have no doubt that by long-continued exposure to tropical heat and malaria the nervous and muscular systems of the heart are relaxed and weakened, becoming thus irritable and defective in contractile power."

Allowing, therefore, that a certain portion of the functional disease of the heart in India may be thus explained, it must not be forgotten that as this condition is very prevalent in the young soldier, it may have been primarily set up before he left his own country.

Syphilis.—That this does directly implicate the heart in some instances there can be no doubt; and in the museum of Netley Hospital there are two good specimens of syphilitic gummata of this organ, and Virchow, Ricord, and others have recorded similar cases; but it is rather with disease of the aorta that this specific poison is connected, and therefore only secondarily with the heart, and to such aortic lesions I shall hereafter refer. It could not, however, be accepted as a marked source of heart disease in the army owing to its great prevalence in the civil population. Dr. Parkes states, in his work on "Hygiène," that "it is quite clear, even admitting its influence, there is no reason to think that syphilis prevails more among soldiers than among the civil male population of the same class." _{Syphilis.} _{Parkes on syphilis.}

Intemperance.—Dr. Maclean (*vide* vol. viii. _{Alcohol.}

Royal United Service Institution Transactions) considers that alcohol exercises a prejudicial influence on the heart and great blood-vessels, but that this can only refer to old soldiers. I think, however, that when taken to excess by young soldiers, although the habit has not become established as a permanent vice, it often produces great injury, by increasing the excitability of the heart's action, which so prevails among them, and to which I shall again draw attention. As regards this vice, however, no great distinction can be drawn between the army and civil population.

It acts prejudicially on the heart of the young and old soldier.

Tobacco.—On this point Dr. Maclean writes:—"Excessive abuse may in many instances result in an irritable condition of the heart, incapacitating a man from much exertion; but I think there is no proof that young soldiers smoke more than other classes of men."

Tobacco (Maclean).

Dr. Chevers, of the Bengal Medical Service (*vide* "A Brief Review of the Means of Preserving the Health of European Soldiers in India," Part I., page 130), states as follows:—"Although instances doubtless occur in which European soldiers, and more especially officers, injure their health by the excessive smoking of tobacco, we have no reason to believe that the practice is ever carried to such an extent in our regiments as to become a distinct element of ill-health. While, however, we doubt the

Tobacco (Chevers).

necessity, or even the possibility, of putting down smoking in the army, it is certain that medical officers in this country (India) will not unfrequently meet with instances in which obstinate indigestion, muscular debility, and functional disorder of the heart are directly attributable to this habit, which must be checked before health can be restored."

That it does not affect to any important extent the hearts of old soldiers or civilians may fairly be surmised, considering that no evidence has been brought forward in support of such a view, though were it correct, it, without doubt, would be easily attainable.

It may, I think, be therefore stated that, though the excesses incidental to the life of the soldier at home and, more especially, on foreign service may contribute in a measure to produce the greater amount of heart disease than is found in the civil population, that they are more than counterbalanced in the latter by the same excesses, coupled with the greater frequency in them of rheumatism and Bright's disease, and consequently that we must look elsewhere for the explanation required. *Vices though tending to produce heart disease cannot be the cause of the excess of the disease in the army.*

Such is undoubtedly the case, and the causes to which I am about to refer have been so fully brought to the notice of the Government, that there is little left me to do but to repeat what has been already written. I allude to the *Special causes have been brought to the notice of the Government.*

32 DISEASES OF THE HEART

particular form of clothing and the amount and arrangement of the accoutrements worn by the soldier when performing exceptional or even ordinary duty.

In civil life all constrictions of clothes removed during exertion.

In civil life, when any prolonged or violent exertion of the body has to be made, be it for pleasure or otherwise, the great point first attended to is to remove all the various constrictions of ordinary dress, it being well known by all classes of society how necessary it is under such circumstances to allow the chest its fullest powers of expansion, and, consequently, the greatest possible freedom to the heart and lungs.

Constriction of neck and chest of soldiers complete.

Now, the method of equipping the soldier is directly opposed to this. His tunic is made to fit as tightly as the skill of the tailor can accomplish, any defect in this respect being probably corrected, after the careful scrutiny of the colonel or adjutant, by a little paring, and finally by the addition of a padded waistcoat, which the soldier takes upon himself to supply.

His waist-belt adds to the constriction below the chest, and his tunic collar above it (with or without the stock), and then, to complete the artificial chest case, the knapsack straps supply all that is requisite, whilst the pouch-belt adds its share to the general compression.

The chest thus fixed as it were in a vice, has

little or no power of expansion, and the circulation through heart, lungs, and great vessels is proportionately impeded.

The constriction of the neck by the tunic collar appears to me to be of more importance than is generally supposed. Fastened as it is by one large hook-and-eye, and fitted closely round the neck, it causes a most marked constriction when the neck becomes distended during exertion, and especially when the knapsack, strapped on, increases the compression antero-posteriorly by drawing the tunic backwards. *Constriction of neck important.*

This constriction must impede the circulation of the blood through the large vessels of the neck, and consequently add greatly to the strain imposed upon the heart by the other portions of the artificial case. The great extent of this compression is easily demonstrated by an examination of the stock or piece of leather worn, for it always bears a deep indentation corresponding to the inward curvature of the hook, which hook is frequently torn away from the collar, although it is sewn to it with special strength. *Evidence of neck compression.*

Referring to the great loss to the army by heart disease, Dr. Maclean (*vide Journal of the Royal United Service Institution*) draws special attention to the mischievous constriction to which soldiers' chests are subjected at the time *Constriction of clothing (Maclean).*

when the maximum of exertion is demanded from them. He writes: "The labouring men have their clothes perfectly free, so do also sportsmen and tourists; but the soldier is compelled to do his work under the utmost possible disadvantages as regards the weight he has to carry, the mode of carrying it, and the entire arrangement of his dress and equipment. Many men fall out in a state of extreme distress, and many surgeons assure me that nothing but a strong feeling of *esprit de corps* prevents many more from doing so."

Of this I also have had ample evidence, and, before I had given the subject much attention, I was somewhat surprised to find that most men who fell out at a "field day" did so during a halt, and that some of these were able to ward off the threatening faintness by walking up and down briskly in rear of their company—thus, I presume, stimulating the heart to increased action.

Statement of committee on army heart disease. The statement of the medical members of the Committee (appointed by Government, in 1864, to inquire into the subject) as to the mode in which they supposed diseases of the heart to be produced in the army, was as follows:—

"During exertion the movements of the chest increase greatly, deeper breathings are made, the diameter of the chest enlarges in all directions, causing greater expansion of the lungs; the blood flows much more rapidly, and the changes in it and the evolution of carbonic acid are trebled and quadrupled in amount, and the heart acts much more quickly and forcibly. If anything destroys the equilibrium between the powerful action of the heart and the capacity of the lungs to receive the blood propelled into them by the heart, the necessary consequence is an accumulation of blood in the cavities and walls of the heart, which leads to an imperfect action of that organ, and to organic changes in its cavities and walls." . . . "The young soldier's ribs and breastbone, while still soft and pliable, are prevented from proper movement by tight-fitting clothes, and by the straps of accoutrements and packs. Of these the cross-belt, bearing the pouch, is the most objectionable, as it passes across the chest and impedes the movement forward of the breast-bone. The waist-belt, also, if too tight, hinders the expansion of the lower ribs. The knapsack straps are less hurtful in this way, but they also press to some extent on the collar-bone and first ribs. It will be seen, therefore, that there is a combination of actions all leading to the same result. The mature soldier, with his bones all formed, and his muscles full grown and strong, may, perhaps, bear these constrictions without injury, but not so the young man. It is probable, however, that more or less injury is done to all."

What better evidence could I adduce in support of views I have long held concerning the heart disease of the army, and which are also strongly pressed by Dr. Parkes in his "Manual of Hygiène?"

Constriction of neck avoided in Austrian army.

I am, however, somewhat surprised that the Committee did not lay stress on the constriction of the collar. In the Austrian army this was obviated by the collar being made loose and turned down, the neck being protected by a neckcloth, and the advantage thus gained over our pattern appeared so great to the late Captain Ram, Scots Fusilier Guards, about eight years ago, that he brought it to the notice of the authorities, but without effect. The tunic, however, made to test its appearance when worn by the British soldier, is still preserved.

Though some of the new pattern clothing issued to the Austrian army, and recently shown to me by the Superintendent of the Royal Clothing Factory, Pimlico, has an upright collar, it is made loose, and the hook and eye which fasten it are very small.

Constriction of neck in Prussian army remedied at times.

Again, in the Prussian army, though the collar fastens tightly round the neck, its prejudicial effect is recognised, and I have been informed by Dr. Münnich that there is a general order for it to be unhooked on the march.

Various experiments have been made by army surgeons to prove how great is the strain on the soldier's heart during exertion by an examination of the pulse at various periods, and these prove, as might be expected, that the action of the heart becomes excessively rapid in proportion to the amount of exertion imposed upon it; and when experiments were made at Chatham to ascertain the comparative amount of distress caused by the accoutrements of various European armies, it was unquestionably proved that, though all produced it more or less, ours ranked first in prejudicial effect. *Amount of strain upon the soldier's heart during exertion has been tested.*

In many instances the first-fruits become soon developed in the recruit. At this period of life (say eighteen to twenty), the various epiphyses of the ribs have not commenced to ossify, and there is no ossific union between the bones of the sternum, the fifth bone only becoming joined to the fourth after puberty, the others still later, while at the same time the cartilages of the ribs are soft and yielding (*vide* Quain's "Anatomy," and Aitken on "Growth of the Recruit," &c). Consequently, constriction of the chest before this has been converted into a firm protecting case for the heart and lungs could not be otherwise *Causes of early development of heart disease in the recruit.*

than prejudicial, and its effect on the recruit is doubly marked if he be of slight frame. The heart also, it must be remembered, has not at this age attained to its full growth; for, according to Boyd, its average weight in males from fourteen to twenty is 7·61 oz., and from twenty to thirty, 10·06 oz.; and therefore this organ, unable to cope with the difficulties suddenly imposed upon it, takes on an irritability or excitability of action which gradually becomes more apparent as the cause is continued.

At first functional derangement of heart.

After a time, owing to the normal growth of the heart, this functional derangement may subside in some cases; but in others it becomes so markedly developed that the sufferer, no longer able to struggle through his duties, is compelled to seek advice.

He then generally states that when at rest he feels perfectly well, and has little or no sensation of throbbing in his chest; so soon, however, as he puts on his tunic and accoutrements and begins his drill, this throbbing occurs with more or less violence, accompanied with a feeling of oppression in that region, and with difficulty of breathing; and this being followed shortly by a sensation of faintness, sickness, or dizziness, he has to fall out of the ranks.

Rest and treatment in hospital for a time may

keep this palpitation within certain limits, but should these means prove unsuccessful the patient must be invalided, although as yet the disease is only purely functional.

On examination at this time percussion reveals little or no increase of cardiac dulness: the sounds of the heart are short and abrupt, the second being abnormally distinct, the apex beat is visible below the left nipple, and the pulse is small and very rapid.

The Committee, to whom I have already referred, in drawing attention to this condition, stated—"The special heart disease from which the young soldier suffers is not, we are informed, disease of the valves, but an extreme excitability of the heart, combined with some, but not great, enlargement. During rest a heart of this kind beats easily, but on the least exertion its action becomes irregular, and the man becomes breathless." *Statement of committee regarding heart disease in the young soldiers.*

The heart at this time not being fully developed, its hypertrophy cannot be easily recognised, and I am inclined to think that this permanent irritability is much dependent on the partial absence of hypertrophy; dilatation of one or more cavities, however, ere long becomes apparent.

It occurred to me that this irritable condition of the heart might be demonstrated by the sphygmograph, and I therefore examined with *The sphygmograph.*

the aid of this instrument the radial pulse of a large number of young soldiers, some suffering from the above, and others in apparent health, but of slight build, and therefore predisposed to it, and I found that, though the various tracings thus obtained presented a great variation both in the force and frequency of the pulse, there was one feature common to all, and to which I wish now to draw special attention, as I cannot find any previous reference made to it in connection with the soldier. I refer to the more or less marked dicrotism present in each specimen.

Its special value in the diagnosis of functional disease of heart in the young soldier.

Sphygmograph (Sanderson).

Dr. Sanderson, in a paper on the sphygmograph in the *British Medical Journal* of July, 1867, writes—" If we can ascertain by the examination of the pulse that the heart is overtaxed long before any change can be detected by auscultation or percussion, it is obvious we have made a step forward in practical utility."

Again, in his lecture on the sphygmograph at the College of Physicians in March, 1867, he stated with reference to dicrotism, that " as a general principle the greater the irregularity of tension produced at the moment of the contraction of the heart between the peripheral arteries and the great trunks, the stronger is the second beat as compared with the first."

He then referred to a tracing of a markedly dicrotic pulse to illustrate one of nervous excitement in a youth, aged eighteen, as a type of merely functional disorder, and stated—"The pyrexial sharpness with which the heart contracted showed itself in an excessively sudden increase of arterial tension, which, in consequence of the great yieldingness of the arteries, was of short duration. The closure of the aortic valves was immediately followed by a diastolic wave of great intensity."

Marey and Naumann also consider that this dicrotism is in a measure due to the recoil of the blood against the closed aortic valves.

Such is undoubtedly my opinion of the cause of the dicrotism in the young soldier. His heart, in its abnormal state of excitability, propels the blood onwards with an unwonted force, and this, returning with unnatural abruptness on the closed valves of the aorta, gives a second shock to the column of blood to an extent that can now be made apparent to the eye. *Explanation of dicrotism in young soldiers.*

The accompanying tracings are a few of those I have taken, and I should state that the time chosen was the morning, before the men had exerted themselves by drill or other duties, and that some of the most marked instances of dicrotism were those of men who were then suffering from the irritability of heart to which I have been alluding. It appears to me that the sphygmograph might thus be very useful as an aid in the diagnosis of doubtful cases of heart irritability in the army, and more especially as a check to the inordinate strain imposed upon this organ by the drills and duties of the recruit, for, according to my observations, it does exactly what Dr. Sanderson expected—viz., proves that the heart is over-taxed long before any change can be detected by auscultation or percussion.

AMONG SOLDIERS. 43

No. 1.—Private L. Aged 20. Service 1 year.

No. 2.—Private W. Aged 19. Service 1 year. P. 160.

No. 3.—Private B. Aged 18¼. Service 1¼ years. P. 110.

No. 4.—Private C. Aged 19¼. Service 1½ years. P. 100.

DISEASES OF THE HEART AMONG SOLDIERS.

No. 5.—Private M. Aged 19¼. Service 1¾ years.

No. 6.—Private W. H. Aged 20. Service 2 years. P. 210.

No. 7.—Private C. W. Aged 23. Service 2 years. P. 110.

No. 8.—Private S. Aged 19¼. Service 2¼ years. P. 160.

DISEASES OF THE HEART AMONG SOLDIERS. 47

No. 9.—Private H. Aged 22. Service 2½ years.

No. 10.—Private G. Aged 21. Service 3 years. P. 10.

No. 11.—Private T. Aged 21. Service 3 years.

No. 12.—Private W. T. Aged 21. Service 3½ years. P. 220.

NOTE.—Since the decision of the Committee, I have reduced the number of tracings to twelve, considering that these are sufficient for publication. They are arranged according to length of service of each soldier. P. means pressure, calculated in grammes.—*Marey's Sphygmograph.*

I do not doubt that there are other causes of this functional derangement of the heart in the army besides what I have already mentioned, such as excessive use of tobacco and spirituous liquors, sexual intercourse, self-indulgence, &c., but these apply in an equal, if not greater, degree to the civil population. *Other causes of functional derangement of heart.*

Dr. Fuller, in his work on "Diseases of the Chest," has entered very fully into the subject of functional derangement of the heart, and at page 626 he writes—"The palpitation itself is often greater than that which accompanies disease of the heart." . . . "The sounds of the heart, unless modified by pre-existing disease, are simply louder, clearer, and more abrupt than natural; but not unfrequently the first sound attains a metallic quality at the apex, and may even be reduplicated, or the second may be reduplicated at the base. This metallic ringing quality of the first sound is characteristic of excessive cardiac excitement, and is doubtless attributable to the energy of the muscular contraction, and the consequently increased tension of the auriculo-ventricular valves." *Functional derangement (Fuller).*

Passing on now from the recruit to the young soldier, I am of opinion that many of these men who suffer from functional disease of the heart soon after joining, find that it passes off after a time, and they are able at last to perform their duties, fully equipped, *Functional derangement may pass off.*

without a feeling of oppression of the chest. But what has taken place? The heart has, undoubtedly, in most cases become increased in bulk, and is thus able to use greater force in the propulsion of the blood, and this hypertrophy when very marked, and accompanied, as almost invariably it is, with dilatation, becomes itself an accepted disease, and one by which, as already shown, the army suffers great loss.

<small>It may pass on to hypertrophy.</small>

When examining the army statistics of "Hypertrophia Cordis," some allowance must probably be made for incompleteness of diagnosis; but it is surely a fact, somewhat remarkable, that in 1860 twenty-three deaths were recorded from this disease among the troops serving in the United Kingdom.

<small>Death from Hypertrophia Cordis.</small>

Dr. Van der Byl (*vide* a paper on "Hypertrophia Cordis," Vol. IX., *Pathological Transactions*,) refers to seventy specimens of this disease he had examined, in only eight of which were all the valves healthy; and also to forty previously published in the *Pathological Transactions*, in all of which the valves were affected.

<small>Van der Byl on "Hypertrophia Cordis."</small>

If, however, the annual death-rate from "Hypertrophia Cordis" is not large, the invaliding for the same is enormous, and it proves, beyond a doubt, that there is a great abnormal strain imposed upon the heart by the life of the soldier.

<small>Invaliding for Hypertrophia Cordis very great.</small>

In civil life hypertrophy, however, is not

uncommon. It is found in all classes of men who undergo extreme muscular exertion, and is in them easy of explanation. It is a frequent result of disease of the kidneys, as I have already shown. It is a necessary sequel of disease of the valves and arterial coats, and of aortic aneurism; and, indeed, of diseases of any other organs or structures which impede, to any extent, the circulation. *[Causes of Hypertrophia Cordis in civil population.]*

If, then, impediments to the circulation can within the body produce hypertrophy of the heart, the same can most certainly be developed by obstructions from without, and especially by such as result from the clothing and accoutrements of our army.

The spirometer is very useful in testing to some extent how much this external compression checks the full expansion of the lungs. *[Spirometer.]*

By experiments I have made with this apparatus, I find that soldiers standing at "attention" with their tunics buttoned up, but *without* their accoutrements, suffered even then a loss of twenty cubic inches on each full inspiration; and, therefore, if the lungs cannot have free play, the heart must also proportionately suffer. *[Its use.]*

In civil life disease of the valves is found to be a very frequent cause of heart-hypertrophy. It was originally stated by Senac ("Maladies du Cœur," tom. I., p. 406), and confirmed more recently by many observers, *[Hypertrophia Cordis caused by a force acting à tergo.]*

among whom may be mentioned Morgagni, Forget, Stokes, Corvisart and Williams, that hypertrophy with dilatation acknowledge as their cause a force acting *à tergo*, attempting to overcome an obstacle in advance, and are attributable to a great extent to valve disease. (*Vide* Dr. Sibson's Report in *Medico-Chirurgical Review*, October, 1854).

All cases of Hypertrophia Cordis in army probably are not diagnosed.

However open to criticism may be the statistics regarding "Hypertrophia Cordis" *per se*, I am quite certain that a very large number of men must be invalided for this condition without having any other form of disease capable of being diagnosed, and I am equally sure, that a far greater number of soldiers have hypertrophied hearts than these cases at all represent, who are able to struggle through their service without passing into that state in which continuance at their duties is no longer possible. This, however, cannot be proved by post-mortem records; for, although the measurements and weight of the hearts of all men who die at Netley are accurately taken, these furnish no proof of what was the condition of the heart previous to the man becoming reduced by some wasting disease to which death is generally attributable in that hospital. In healthy men, with well-formed chests, the impulse of the heart is felt between the fifth and sixth ribs to right of left nipple, and one to two inches below it, and, excepting in thin men is not generally visible; pulsation of carotids can sometimes be seen—of subclavians rarely, and of radials still more rarely.

Examine, however, the soldier of six, eight, or ten years' service when he should be in the prime of life, and how rarely will such a state be found! As a rule, it is far otherwise. There is a fulness of the præcordial region, the apex beat is generally distinctly visible, its impulse is heaving, and felt over a larger surface and lower down than in health; pulsation is also often visible in the epigastric region, and the sounds of the heart are rather muffled. Visible pulsation in the carotids is frequently very marked, in subclavians to a less extent, and in radials by no means rarely, and its force, as shown by the sphygmograph, is exaggerated.

Enlargement of heart evident in many soldiers of some years' service.

Dr. Aitken states (*vide* "Practice of Medicine,") that "increased impulse of the heart is generally due to some morbid state of the heart itself. It is stronger than natural in hypertrophy of the walls of the left ventricle, and is greatest in hypertrophy with dilatation of the ventricles. In such cases the impulse is slow, gradual, heaving, double, and occasionally so violent as to shake the bed on which the patient rests. This slow, progressive heaving impulse is produced by no other cause than

Impulse of the heart (Aitken).

hypertrophy with dilatation of the ventricles of the heart; and in such cases the extent of surface over which the impulse is felt is much increased. In hypertrophy of the left ventricle with dilatation of its cavity the impulse is felt lower down, more to the left side, and over a very much larger surface than natural."

This condition is, therefore, very similar to what, as I have just stated, is found in the soldier after some years' service, in whom, by himself at least, no disease is suspected.

Although I have not specially referred to dilatation of the left ventricle, I have no doubt that it is frequently present with hypertrophy, and is sometimes the most marked where the muscular structure is soft, and consequently more yielding.

<small>Hypertrophy (Fuller).</small> Dr. Fuller (*vide* "Diseases of the Heart," p. 573), writes—"Hypertrophy is, in most instances, accompanied by dilatation, and involves both sides of the heart, the left being that on which the hypertrophy is most apparent; but when it is local, its most common seat is the left ventricle, next the right ventricle, next the left auricle, and lastly, the right auricle. The causes of hypertrophy, whatever their precise nature, have one element in common; they all operate as incentives to increased cardiac action. This, in truth, is their essential character. Without an increased demand

on the force of the heart's action hypertrophy would never arise, whereas it is an intelligible and necessary result of any long-continued and abnormally forcible cardiac pulsation. Hence it is that hypertrophy implies the existence of obstruction to the current of the blood, for in such cases the heart is stimulated to increased exertion with a view to adapt itself to the altered mechanism of the circulation, and the result of that unwonted force of action is the same in the heart as in other muscles—viz., increased development of structure."

He then states the various causes of hypertrophy, of which I may mention "continued and inordinate use of stimulants, excessive and violent bodily exercise, disease of the valves, constriction of vessels consequent upon pressure from without or on deposit within their coats, dilatations of vessels, aneurism, or otherwise," these being of special importance to the army.

I shall now pass on to valvular disease of the heart in the army; but here I am met by a great difficulty—viz., a defective nomenclature, for the published statistics embrace diseases of the various valves under the general term of "morbus valvularum cordis." Even if this were not the case, the diagnosis in a large number of men might be open to doubt, not so much with reference to aortic or mitral valve disease alone, as to their detection when co-

Valvular diseases.

Difficulty in sub-dividing them, owing to statistics.

Diagnosis liable to error.

existent—the presence of the one being marked by the more prominent evidences of the other; but even with regard to aortic valve disease, I think it highly probable that, in some instances, a bruit heard over the base of the heart is attributed to this cause, whereas its actual production is due to the blood flowing over a roughened aortic lining membrane near the valves, a condition so often found in dead soldiers.

Maclean.

Dr. Maclean lays great stress on the fact that great numbers of men are admitted into the wards of Netley Hospital for "morb. valv. cordis," in whom no such disease exists, and who are suffering from functional disorder of the heart alone.

Morehead.

Dr. Morehead (*vide* "Remarks on the Diseases of India") states also, that by carefully examining the invalids sent to Bombay with "disease of the heart," in several he found it did not exist.

Post-mortem give very certain proofs.

I, therefore, should feel much doubt as to the truthfulness of any evidence I could adduce from invaliding records of the relative extent of aortic and mitral disease in the army.

Post-mortem records, however, are not open to this objection, and I have, therefore, carefully examined those available at Netley Hospital, in order that I might obtain a fair estimate on this point, and I cannot imagine that any records exist elsewhere which could furnish me, though on a small scale, with better materials for this inquiry.

By these I find as follows:— *Statistics of aortic and mitral valve disease. Deaths—army. Aortic most common.*

Aortic Valve disease.	Mitral Valve disease.	Aortic & Mitral Valve disease.
50	25	22
	Total 97	

This number includes cases recorded in the post-mortem returns from October, 1860, to November, 1869, and has reference as well to the pathological specimens previously existing, and it shows clearly that aortic is much more prevalent than mitral valve disease in the army. Dr. Maclean (*vide* "Army Medical Report, 1867,") found also, that his clinical records at Netley gave an excess of aortic valve disease, though not to the same extent, thus:—

Total cases.	Aortic Valve disease.	Mitral Valve disease.
126	72	54

Statistics of same. Invaliding—army. Aortic most common.

The relative frequency of the disease of these valves in civil life has been specially studied by Drs. Barclay, Chambers, and Ormerod (*vide British and Foreign Medico-Chirurgical Review*, Vol. xiv.) with this result, viz:—

Total cases.	Aortic Valve disease.	Mitral Valve disease.	Aortic & Mitral Valve disease.
673	192	205	259

Statistics of same. Civil population. Mitral more common than aortic.

Showing that disease affects both valves in the greater number of cases, and that the mitral are more frequently attacked than the aortic. Other statistics are given to prove that, when associated with acute rheumatism, disease affects both valves in the greater number of cases, and the mitral more frequently than the aortic.

<small>Aortic valve disease more common than mitral valve disease in army (Lawson).</small>

Dr. Lawson has pointed out the greater frequency of aortic than mitral valve disease in the army (*vide* Army Medical Report, 1866), and this is also shown, though on a very small scale, by the records (post-mortem) of my regiment; thus, between February 1861 and 1869 there have been seven instances of aortic valve disease, one of mitral and aortic (this case and one of the others having been probably set up by acute rheumatism), but no case of mitral disease alone.

Accepting it, then, as a fact that aortic valve disease is more frequently found in the army than mitral valve disease, and that the reverse holds good in the civil population, I shall now proceed to point out to what have been ascribed the affections of the aortic valves.

<small>Causes of aortic valve disease (Peacock).</small>

Dr. Peacock (*vide* "Lectures on Valvular Diseases of the Heart"), after giving some statistics, writes:—"These facts show the influence of over-exertion as an exciting cause of aortic valvular disease, whatever may be the circumstances which predispose to this affection.". . . "Men are shown by the table to be much more subject to valvular disease than women, but though the difference to the disadvantage of men obtains in all forms of valvular affections, it operates to a much greater extent in cases of aortic valvular disease than in any of the other forms." . . . "It is evident, therefore, that the greater prevalence of valvular disease in males than in females is chiefly due to the greater frequency in the former of aortic valvular affections. This is doubtless the result of the liability of the aortic valves in men to injury from accident or over-exertion, and to the more common occurrence of various febrile affections, originating in cold, intemperance, &c., in men than in women."

If, therefore, as I have tried to prove, hypertrophy of the heart, so common in the army, has for its chief cause a too great strain on its powers by the life of the soldier, and if, as Dr. Peacock says, over-exertion will produce disease of the aortic rather than of the mitral valves, then surely it may be inferred that the great prevalence of diseases of these valves in particular may in part be thus explained.

Further, hypertrophy of the heart, when this is a primary lesion, must in some cases be the cause of disease of the aortic valves, for the increased force with which the blood, propelled by a heart in this condition, recoils upon them, must produce an abnormal strain, and thus tend to induce thickening, and ultimately many of the various diseased conditions in which they are found after death. Mr. Wearne, Assistant Professor of Pathology at

Hypertrophy of heart may precede the valve disease.

Netley, informs me that in the post-mortem examinations made at that hospital it is of most common occurrence to find the aortic valves thickened.

Dilatation may precede valve disease.

Again, when hypertrophy is accompanied by much dilatation the aortic orifice most probably would also be dilated, owing to the close connection of this vessel with the ventricle, and then the valves, no longer able to close the abnormally large aperture, must allow regurgitation, which in its turn must tend to produce disease of their structure by the consequent friction, without inflammation being necessarily present.

Friction alone can induce disease of valves without inflammation.

That friction alone can induce disease of the valves has been long pointed out.

Some authors, as M. Bouillaud, in 1824, in his conjoint work with M. Bertin, have considered morbid depositions in the coats of the arteries to be in every case the various metamorphoses of lymph effused by inflammation; but more recently M. Bouillaud qualified his original opinion, which disclaimed any agency but inflammation, and thus wrote (*Traité* ii., p. 309):—"It appears to me probable that the perpetual friction to which the valves and arterial walls are subjected is really a physiological or functional condition which ought not to be overlooked in determining all the circumstances calculated to favour the development of

Opinion of Bouillaud on same.

certain indurations of these parts, cartilaginous or osseous." And Dr. Hope, in commenting upon the above, added (*vide* "Diseases of the Heart," 4th edition, p. 213):—"In admitting that these structural changes may occur independent of inflammation, M. Bouillaud admits as much as I have ever contended for in this volume, and as much as Audral contends for."

I have lately had under my care two typical cases of this form of heart disease, viz., disease of the aortic valves with hypertrophy, having the following history:—

Both patients were temperate, married men, of good character, and of nearly twenty years' service. They considered themselves in excellent health, but my attention was drawn to them about the same time by their anxious expression of countenance as indicative of heart disease. On examination, I found that both were suffering from extensive hypertrophy of the heart, with very marked aortic valvular disease, but with no apparent affection of the other valves. The sphygmographic tracings Nos. 49 and 50 show how great was the regurgitation in each case. Dr. Sibson, who most carefully examined these men, agreed with me that, in all probability, the disease commenced as hypertrophy, induced by some abnormal obstruction to the circulation, and that the valve disease was secondary to it.

Record of two cases of heart hypertrophy followed by valve disease.

These cases represent a form of disease which is rarely found in the civil population, but which I believe is by no means uncommon in the army—viz., disease of the aortic valves, and of these valves only, secondary to hypertrophy of the left ventricle, and without any known history of disease to account for this hypertrophy; whereas, in the civil population, disease of the aortic valves alone is uncommon, as already shown, and when existing is found to precede, and not to follow, the hypertrophy.

Syphilis, again, must not be omitted as one cause of valve disease, and especially as when once it has thoroughly impregnated the system, no part of the body is certain of escape from its ravages; but I believe its effect on the valves is not great.

Therefore, admitting an equal proportion of aortic valve disease in the army and civil population due to the same causes, I would attribute the excess found in the former to hypertrophy, passing on to this more serious lesion as above explained, and to the great and constant strain imposed upon these valves by the excessive recoil of the blood when there is some abnormal check to the circulation.

In proceeding now to refer to aneurism and diseases of the coats of the aorta, my remarks will occupy a considerable portion of this essay, for these diseases are so blended with those of the heart proper, both as regards cause and effect, that I consider their study to be absolutely inseparable. *Aneurism.*

Aneurism of the heart, either in the army or civil population, is of such rare occurrence that it needs but a passing comment. *Aneurism of heart.*

Mr. Thurnam (*vide Medico-Chirurgical Transactions*, vol. 21, p. 227, 1858), in his elaborate essay on "Aneurism of the Heart," records fifty-eight cases of this disease; but in seventeen only of this number was he able to obtain information as to the occupation and mode of life of the sufferers. Of these seventeen cases he writes: "It is a striking fact, that out of this number, eight, or about one-half, should have been soldiers, a circumstance which would lead one to suspect that exposure—to which *Mr. Thurnam.*

this class of persons is subject—and the forced exercise they undergo, may have something to do with the production of this lesion."

Aneurisms of heart in Netley records. In the records of Netley Hospital, I have found six cases of this disease, one of which is included in Mr. Thurnam's seventeen, and also two which were situated in the sinuses of Valsalva, and implicated the left ventricle.

Aneurism of thoracic aorta. Aneurism of the thoracic aorta, though now so frequently found in the army, has only of late years much attracted the attention of military surgeons. In 1836, the late Dr. Hunter made a passing allusion to it, as I shall presently show, and this is the earliest observation I can find of its prevalence in the army.

Scarpa on aneurism. According to Scarpa, it was not until the year 1557 that any certain knowledge was obtained with regard to the existence of internal aneurisms; Vesalius then pointed out this disease in the person of Leonard Velserus, in whom, after a fall from a horse, a pulsating tumour had appeared in the back, near to the spine. And even in the year 1670, when Elsnerus published the observations of Riva with regard to aneurism of the arch of the aorta, he prefixed to these observations the title, "*De paradoxico aneurysmate aortæ.*" Such are the earliest records of the disease.

Great prevalence of aneurism in the army (Lawson). In 1866, Inspector-General Lawson proved by statistics that deaths from aortic aneurism were eleven times more numerous in the army than in the male civil population (*vide* "Army Medical Report," 1866); but deaths from this disease give no real estimate of its relative extent in the two classes, for, like soldiers suffering from heart disease, many must leave the service thus affected and die ultimately from the same, their deaths being recorded in the civil statistics. In illustration of this, Mr. Muscroft, of Pontefract, has informed me that, as Poor Law Medical Officer, he has had several cases of aneurism under his care, all of which were in discharged soldiers.

Statistics of death not alone sufficient for comparison with civil population.

Muscroft.

As its comparatively great prevalence in the army may now be looked upon as an established fact (*vide Lancet*, February 20, 1869), statistics in proof thereof are scarcely necessary; but I think the following have some interest attaching to them:—

Statistics of Aneurism in the Army, Navy, and Civil Population of London.

Aneurism in army and navy and civil population.

		Strength.	Deaths. Ratio per 1,000.
1862 to 1865 (4 years)	Army—(Foot Guards and Line in United Kingdom)	176,390	·36
	Navy	217,170	·1
1861	Civil Population ...	507,405	·09
1860 to 1866 (7 years)	White Troops—(Cape of Good Hope) ...	29,930	·9
1860 to 1866 (7 years)	White Troops—(New Zealand)	42,462	·7

These statistics include all aneurisms, owing

to the impossibility of treating them otherwise; but they may be fairly considered to apply to the aorta to a far greater extent than to any other vessel or vessels.

Causes of Aneurism.

Causes of aneurism (Corvisart).

Corvisart thus writes (in his treatise on "Diseases of the Heart," p. 318, A.D. 1811):—
"Aneurism may be produced by two causes; firstly, the increased impelling force of the blood; and secondly, impediments to the circulation situated beyond the dilated part. The increase of the muscular force of the heart destroys the harmony which should exist between that organ and the aorta, into the cavity of which it sends the blood with too much impetuosity. The coats of the artery insensibly yield to the powerful impetus of the blood, and this ever-acting cause induces the dilatation."

Causes of aneurism (Reeder).

Again, Dr. Reeder (*vide* "Practical Treatise on the Inflammatory and Organic Diseases of Heart," &c., p. 256, A.D. 1821,) thus writes:—
"The uniform dilatation of all the coats of the aorta, must be attributed to a loss in their tone or natural power of resistance; or, sometimes, though they possess their natural strength, the blood is propelled into the thoracic aorta with such an augmented momen-

tum, in consequence of great corporeal exertion or vehement mental emotion, that it may not be able to withstand its impetus, and therefore dilates." . . . . "Or, sometimes, very vehement action of the blood, external violence, or great and sudden bodily exertion, may produce rupture of the internal and middle tunics, and hence aneurism, when no morbid state previously existed."

Similar views of the causes of aneurism in the civil population are still generally held, and as the case recorded by Vesalius, in 1557, originated in a fall, so may many which occur in the present day, be traced to a like cause. When recently examining the "post-mortem" records of St. George's Hospital, by the kind permission of the Medical School Committee, I particularly remarked that a large number of the thoracic aneurisms were stated to have arisen from severe falls or accidents of some kind.

Now, to what is due the great prevalence of aortic aneurism in the army? Syphilis, that scourge of the army, naturally occurs to the mind as the probable explanation thereof; and Dr. Aitken, at least, evidently holds this view, for in his "Practice of Medicine," he reports twenty-four cases examined by him at Netley, in seventeen of which number he found cicatricial-like loss of substance of the inner coat of the aorta; and this condition

The effect of syphilis on aortic coats (Aitken).

he attributed to syphilis, there having been in each case a distinct history of the same, associated with unmistakeable syphilitic lesions in other organs. Without doubt, this is strong evidence in support of his opinion, but the following statement is evidence, even more marked, to the contrary effect.

Maclean. Dr. Maclean writes (*vide* Annual Report for 1867, p. 301):—" Between April 1, 1867, and April 1, 1869, thirty-six cases of aneurism of the aorta were under treatment in the clinical wards of Netley." . . . " The Medical History Sheets showed a rheumatic history in five, and a distinct syphilitic history in only three of the cases." . . . " The evidence furnished from this hospital, and the careful inquiries of the Pack Committee, point unequivocally to dress and accoutrements as the active agents in this distressing amount of mischief." I cannot believe that syphilis plays more than a minor part in the production of aortic aneurism. When, however, syphilis attacks the coats of the aorta it must, without doubt, like atheromatous disease, so diminish the natural elasticity of this vessel as to favour the development of an aneurism; and therefore, whatever would cause an aneurismal dilatation of the aorta without syphilis would certainly be greatly aided by it.

According to the statistics of Dr. Davidson,

to which I shall again refer, syphilitic disease of the aortic coats is by no means uncommon; but if, as Dr. Parkes* and others state, this specific disease is nearly, or quite, as common in the lower classes of the civil population as in the army, then, to attribute the excess of aneurism in the army to this cause must surely be wrong, for no class of men is so favourably placed as the soldier for the early and careful treatment of its primary and secondary lesions. *(Syphilitic disease of aortic coats (Davidson).)*

The same remarks apply to the excessive use of spirits, this vice without doubt tending to cause a deterioration of the aortic coats.

Concerning this, Dr. Carpenter thus writes (*vide* "Prize Essay on the Use and Abuse of Alcoholic Liquors in Health and Disease," 1850):—"The continued but irregular excitement of the contractile action of the heart and arteries, which is the result of the habitual use of stimulants, must of itself predispose these tissues to disease; and this predisposition will of course be increased by the contact of blood, charged with alcohol, with their lining membrane, as well as by the general disordered condition of their nutritive operations. Now, attacks of acute arteritis seem not unfrequently traceable to alcoholic intoxication; and it cannot therefore be regarded as improbable that those more chronic disorders of their walls *(Effect of spirits on the heart.)*

* *Vide* page 29.

which give rise to aneurism, softening, fatty degeneration, and other structural changes, and which thereby predispose to hæmorrhage, should be favoured, if not absolutely produced, by the presence of alcohol in the circulating fluid."

Granting, then, that syphilis and excess of alcohol may account for a certain number of the aortic aneurisms of the army, I would assign the production of the majority to mechanical obstruction to the circulation in the soldier when he is undergoing exertion, caused by the general constriction of his neck and chest by faulty clothing and accoutrements.

<small>A special cause of aneurism.</small>

The heart, as I have already pointed out, to overcome its difficulties, becomes frequently hypertrophied; but the aorta has not the same power. The blood, propelled with great force by the left ventricle, and checked in its onward flow, produces a great strain on the thoracic aorta, and by frequently dilating it beyond its normal limits, must ultimately so weaken, or even lacerate, the elastic fibres of the middle coat as to allow of the formation of an aneurism, or of a permanent dilatation, in that part of the vessel where the shock is most felt—viz., the ascending and transverse portion of the arch.

<small>The aorta is over dilated.</small>

In 1728, Nicholls on several occasions performed the experiment, before the Royal Society of London (*vide* "Philosophical Trans-

<small>Experiments of Nicholls.</small>

actions," A.D. 1728), of forcing fluid into the aorta, and thus rupturing the inner and middle coats at some points, caused a swelling of the cellular sheath similar to an aneurismal tumour; and Scarpa, in comparing the different elasticity of the arteries and veins, stated that it was easily understood why, on account of the rigidity and brittleness of the proper arterial coats, and of the kind of contact which existed between them, the fibres of their muscular membrane were more disposed to be ruptured from the violent impetus of the blood than the veins.

If aneurisms of the aorta are produced by the force of the blood, it cannot be doubted that their most frequent situation must be in that portion of the aorta which has to bear the greatest strain; and such is precisely the case.

Dr. Sibson, in his "Medical Anatomy," records 703 cases of aortic aneurism, of which number 420 involved some portion of the ascending aorta; and he concludes that these tumours most frequently arise from that part of the vessel against which the greatest force of the blood is directed. *Situation of aneurisms (Sibson).*

Now, if this view be correct, and if it be true that the circulation in the soldier is more subject to mechanical obstruction than in the civilian, then the site of this disease in the soldier should specially corroborate the result of Dr. Sibson's investigations; and that it does so I can by the following statistics prove:—

Army statistics strengthen those of Sibson.

Ascending aorta	Arch.	Descending aorta	Thoracic aorta	Abdominal aorta	Total.
37	38	12	7	15	= 109.

Or, ascending aorta and arch, 75; other thoracic, 19.

The records at my disposal do not permit me to give more definite sites to these aneurisms than as above, but they show how great is the proportion involving the two first-named divisions of the vessel.

These cases have been abstracted from the post-mortem and museum records of Netley Hospital, care having been taken to exclude some which were not of soldiers, and from the post-mortem records of my own regiment since 1861.

Though no notice was taken apparently of the views of Dr. Hunter, 2nd Queen's, on the cause of heart and aortic disease in the army, when, in 1836, he published them in the first volume of the "Transactions of the Medical and Physical Society of Bombay," they were very similar to those now held by many army surgeons. He thus wrote:—"Whether or not rheumatism be the first link in this morbid chain, a more sufficient cause for hastening its progress, I am convinced, is the active duty a soldier undergoes whilst buttoned up in his accoutrements. These, by compressing the

Cause of aneurism in army (Hunter).

neck andchest, obstru ct the circulation to such a degree as to excite the heart to inordinate action, and cause great hypertrophy in the strong and muscular, and dilatation in the weak and sickly. Again, in the former the natural resiliency of the aorta being overcome by the inordinate force of the circulation, that vessel yields, dilates, and finally gives way, giving rise to aneurism."

In 1867, Staff-Surgeon Hyde published the report of a case of aortic aneurism (*vide* "Army Medical Report," 1867), to which he appended the following remarks:— "The absence of atheroma in the coats deserves notice; it will probably be evolved, as these cases are more observed, that numerous instances of aortic aneurism in the army are unconnected with any special pre-existing structural degeneration of the arterial system; that they frequently commence under strain as sacculated projecting pouches of the entire vascular coating."

Hyde.

The statistics of aneurism in the army and navy, which I have given at page 65, are, I think, of great importance in support of the opinion, that mechanical obstruction to the circulation must be the chief cause of the disease, for though it is more prevalent in the army, it is in the navy considered to be very common; and Mr. Harry Leech, in referring to the large number of cases the *Dreadnought* furnishes, thus writes (*vide* " Pathological Transactions," 1865):— " The great exertions made whilst leaning bodily over the yards in reefing, hauling at ropes, and lifting heavy weights, are among the chief causes producing aneurismal dilatations in sailors." But however violent their work may be, there is no mechanical obstruction to their circulation by tight clothing, &c., and consequently they suffer less from aneurism than the army; whereas, if constitutional syphilis were the main exciting cause of aneurism, the navy should not suffer less than the army from the one, having an equal share of the other disease. The very high ratio of deaths from aneurism among the troops in New Zealand and the Cape of Good Hope during the period 1860-1866, I would attribute to the great fatigues and long marches to which they were there subjected.

Taking, then, into consideration all the various facts and opinions I have collected, and the many cases of the disease which have come under my immediate notice, I am confident that what I have above stated is the true explanation of the excess of aortic aneurism in the army.

Closely connected with aneurism, and, like it, of great importance to my subject in being a not unfrequent cause of hypertrophy of the heart, is disease of the coats of the aorta. To this I shall now proceed to allude, and in the first place may state my belief that very few specimens of thoracic aortas in a perfectly normal condition are to be found in soldiers who have died after eight or ten years' service.

The late Dr. Todd (*vide* "Cyclopædia of Anatomy and Physiology," p. 224), when referring to the structure of the coats of arteries, thus wrote :—" It is the external tunic in which the power of resistance in the longitudinal direction resides; the resistance in the circular direction is much greater, and is owing to the middle and external tunics conjointly; the internal tunic has very little power of resistance in either direction. The middle and internal tunics are as remarkable for their fragility as the external is for its toughness and power of resistance." Then, in pointing out the deviation in the aorta from the cylindrical form of arteries, and the dilatation on the right side of the ascending limb of the arch at its junction with the transverse, he stated :— "This dilatation, which did not exist in the fœtus, grows larger as life advances, and appears to be produced by the impulse of the blood." Therefore, even in the normal condition of a man, the force with which blood passes through the aorta has a tendency to injure this vessel; and indeed, Nature has apparently foreseen this, for, according to Haller, the

[margin: Todd on structure of aorta, &c.]

convex is thicker than the concave border of the arch.

<small>Causes of disease of aortic coats.</small> Putting aside the atheromatous disease, &c., of the aorta which is frequently found in the bodies of old persons, I would chiefly attribute the abnormal condition of this vessel, so common in the army, to two causes—viz., syphilis, and mechanical obstruction to the circulation; and these, though very different in themselves, produce somewhat similar results.

<small>Morgagni.</small> Morgagni has noticed the influence of syphilis in producing structural change in the aortic coats; but, on the other hand, I can find no <small>Virchow.</small> mention of syphilis by Virchow, in his "Cellular Pathology," as a cause of the atheroma, calcification and ossification of the aorta.

<small>Hope.</small> Dr. Hope thus wrote on disease of arterial valves and coats (*vide* "Diseases of Heart," p. 211, 4th edition):—" It appears to me that over-distention of the arteries and their valves by the force of the circulation, is what principally, at least, produces this effect." Among other reasons for this view, he gave the arterial ossifications found in stags long and often exercised in running, and not in those which lead a tranquil life (Boerhaave); the greater amount of diseases of the arteries and aneurism in men than in women (at least seven or eight to one), the life of the former being much more laborious, and the circulation more liable to excite-

ment from potation of vinous and spirituous liquors; the greater frequency of ossifications of those arteries most exposed to over-distention —viz., the arch of the aorta and the arteries of the brain, &c. He then added: "Perhaps the same reason—viz., over-distention—may be assigned for the remarkable frequency of the arterial depositions in those who have suffered much from syphilis or mercury, for, as these maladies induce a cachectic state, which lessens the elasticity of all the tissues, the arterial tissue would, under such circumstances, suffer proportionately more from the distending pressure of the circulation."

Dr. Davidson (*vide* "Army Medical Report," vol. v. p. 481) states, that in 114 post-mortems at Netley, there were found twenty-two instances of atheroma of the aorta: of the whole 114, in seventy-eight cases without syphilitic history, there were four instances of atheroma; in eight cases, with doubtful syphilitic history, there was one of atheroma; while the remaining twenty-eight cases, in which there was a marked syphilitic history, furnished seventeen instances.

Netley records of syphilitic disease of aorta.

With such evidence, to doubt that syphilis is a great cause of disease in the aorta would scarcely be justifiable.

It probably appears, at first, in the form of a sub-acute inflammation of the inner and middle coat, leading to deposit, in or between them,

Effect of syphilitic disease of coats, &c.

of fibro-plastic material, which subsequently breaks down and passes into granular and fatty degeneration, the result of which is commonly known as atheroma.

Effect of mechanical obstructions.
The effect of mechanical obstruction to the circulation is of a different kind.

As I have already pointed out, the constant over-distention of the aorta by an undue column of blood, propelled probably by an hypertrophied heart, gradually exhausts the elasticity of the inner and middle coats; and the transverse, or rather, oblique fibres of the latter become so over-stretched, weakened, and, in some instances, even lacerated, that they have no longer the power of contracting the vessel to its proper calibre.

When this takes place, the inner coat loses its smoothness, and becomes irregular and corrugated, the corrugations being chiefly longitudinal; and ultimately, the vessel may pass into much the same state of degeneration as in the former case.

Points of difference between effects of syphilis and of mechanical obstruction.
I think, however, some very marked points of difference can be drawn between the two conditions. When the disease is due to syphilis, it is more extensive and not limited to the ascending and transverse portion of the arch of the aorta; the lining membrane is not so distinctly corrugated, but it assumes a worm-eaten appearance, with markings as

if of healed ulcers—occasionally has actual ulcers—and, in some instances, distinct elevations of the inner coat from circumscribed deposits beneath it; this latter condition being specially characteristic of this specific disease.

The frequency with which these lesions, like aneurism, are found in that part of the aorta only which has to bear the greatest strain—viz., from its origin to the junction of the transverse with the descending part of the arch—point to the other cause (over-dilatation), as also the great extent to which the entire circumference of the aorta is sometimes affected from the valves to the aneurism, if there be one, whereas beyond the sac the vessel appears nearly, if not quite, healthy. Of this I have recently seen a few well-marked instances, and more especially one, which was that of a young soldier who never had had syphilis, and in whom the aorta on the proximal side of the aneurism was extremely corrugated, and beyond it quite normal.

Again, the great frequency of disease of the aortic coats in the soldier is opposed to its production mainly by syphilis, for syphilis in a very severe form is not *specially* prevalent in the army, and in its milder forms it cannot be supposed to affect these tissues so markedly.

In some of the most severe cases of syphilis in the post-mortem records of Netley Hospital,

—even to the extent of caries of the cranial bones—the aorta was found free from disease. I cannot, however, obtain from these records what I should consider a satisfactory numerical statement on this point, for, in the earlier records, in many instances of marked syphilitic history, *no* mention is made of the condition of the aorta; and such negative evidence, though possibly implying the absence of disease, is no proof of the aorta having been examined.*

Disease of coats must lead to enlargement of heart.

Disease, however, of the aorta, be its cause what it may, must, like aneurism, compel the heart to use greater exertion to counterbalance the force lost by the want of elasticity of the vessel, and thus tend to cause hypertrophy of this organ.

Latham.

Dr. Latham (*vide* "Clinical Lectures on Diseases of the Heart," vol. ii., p. 211) says: "I believe that a dilatation of the aorta is more apt to disturb the action of the heart and ultimately to injure its structure, when it occurs as a general enlargement of the vessel than as an abrupt expansion in the form of a sac; and I believe also that the nearer it is found to the origin of the aorta, the more capable it is of producing these effects."

* With regard to this point, Dr. Aitken (being one of the examiners of the essays) writes:—"It is always examined, and always has been; but positive, and not negative evidence, alone finds a place in the record. That is the rule."

To the soldier's "spot," to which special attention has been drawn by Drs. Maclean and Aitken, I need not here refer further than to record my recognition of it as one of our best proofs of the frequent presence of an abnormal impediment to the free action of his heart, and my belief that beyond this fact it has no important signification, nor in any way endangers life.   *The soldier's spot.*

To sum up what I have so far written, it may be said that it is an undeniable fact that disease of the heart is more prevalent in the army than in the civil population; that its three main causes, as generally understood— viz., rheumatism, Bright's disease, and violent manual labour—apply more to the latter than to the former; that syphilis, whatever may be its effects on this organ, directly or indirectly, by attacking both classes to nearly the same extent, must produce a relatively equal deteriorating effect; that disease of the mitral is more common than disease of the aortic valves in the civil population, and aortic more than mitral in the army, and consequently, that there must be something specially associated with the life of the soldier to produce this marked difference; that though the heat and malarious diseases of India and of other countries in which our army has to serve may not, according to statistics, produce a greater ratio of   *General summary.*

heart disease than this more healthy climate of Great Britain, it is probable that such is their tendency, as well as to develope more rapidly disease, the foundation of which has been laid in the young soldier before he leaves his own country; that the very frequent functional derangement of the heart of the young soldier can be readily detected by the sphygmograph before it is otherwise recognisable; and, therefore, that this instrument might be made of great use in directing attention to an abnormal condition, which, amenable to treatment at first, is only the precursor, if neglected, of diseases that, though capable of being kept within certain limits, cannot be cured; that there is one special cause of heart disease in our army now clearly laid down by those who have most studied the subject—viz., the prejudicial constriction of the uniform and accoutrements—this producing such obstruction to the circulation that, either directly or indirectly, as by aneurism and disease of the aortic coats, &c., the heart is abnormally strained, and frequently passes into a state of functional derangement, and ultimately of organic disease.

The gradual effect on the heart of this mechanical obstruction may be described as follows:—

So soon as the young peasant leaves the plough, or the mechanic his trade, and is enlisted into the service, an abnormal strain is perpetually thrown on his heart. At first this excites an irritability of action which, in some weakly constitutions, the heart cannot shake off; and thus the man who, a few years before, hardly knew he had a heart, now finds that a violent throbbing in his chest on the slightest exertion has rendered him unfit for the duties of a soldier, and that he must be discharged the service. His heart has, at this time, not passed beyond a state of functional derangement, excepting in some cases where there is, in addition, dilatation of the right cavities.

In a stronger man, the heart does not at once succumb, but by growth gains strength, and is thus able, for a time at least, to overcome its difficulties. This hypertrophy, which affects chiefly the left ventricle, may not become sufficiently great to attract attention, although it may be detected by examination; but, should it become very marked, it may entail the loss of the man to the service by invaliding, or even, in a few instances apparently, by death.

Should neither of these results occur, in a few years another complication may arise—viz., disease of the aortic valves—which must inevitably lead to the same. Then, passing from the heart to the aorta, aneurism and other diseases of its coats clearly point to mechanical obstruction as their chief, *though not only* cause, from the fact of the very great majority of these lesions implicating that part of the vessel which receives the greatest shock from the circulation of the blood.

IV. Measures to check heart disease in the army.

These remarks leave unnoticed only the final division of my subject, and to this I shall now refer—viz., the measures I would propose with a view to check the great loss to the service by these diseases.

This may be divided into curative and preventive. Of the former, little need be said, for, when once established, heart disease is little amenable to *any but palliative* treatment.

Even functional derangement of heart not easy to cure (Maclean).

Even with regard to the functional derangement of the young soldier's heart, Dr. Maclean thus writes (*vide* "Army Medical Report," 1867):—"Once fairly set up, I doubt if it is ever really cured. I have kept young men under observation for months under the most favourable conditions as regards rest, diet, and medicine, but, on causing them to resume their ordinary dress and accoutrements, or to walk quietly about the corridors of the hospital, distressing palpitation immediately returned, making further exertion impossible."

Recovery from simple hypertrophy doubtful (Fuller).

Then, concerning recovery from simple hypertrophy of the heart, Dr. Fuller writes (*vide* "Diseases of the Chest," p. 573):—" My own conviction is, that the complete removal of hypertrophy is well-nigh impossible; but I am fully convinced that, by careful attention to hygienic rules for a lengthened period, its effects may be moderated and kept within such bounds that the patient shall be scarcely conscious of its existence, and shall live on for a long series of years in the enjoyment of tolerable health."

Of the almost absolute uselessness of treatment of chronic valve disease, or of aneurisms of the thoracic aorta, there can also be no doubt; but, however limited our powers may be in the cure of all these diseases, they can be exercised with markedly good effect in their prevention, owing to our complete knowledge of the heart's functions and mechanism. *[margin: Treatment of chronic valve disease useless.]*

"The heart is neither an organ of secretion nor of excretion, and there is scarcely any other whose functions are so purely mechanical" (Wardrop). "It is truly a mechanical engine, for, although the muscles are the powers in an animal, yet these powers are themselves often converted into a machine, of which the heart is a strong instance. For, from the disposition of its muscular fibres, tendons, ligaments, and valves, it is adapted to mechanical purposes, which make it a complete organ or machine in itself" (John Hunter). *[margin: The heart (Wardrop). The heart (Hunter).]*

The directly prejudicial effect on the heart of extremes of climate and malaria, and also of diseases of other organs, consequent upon the *[margin: Injurious effects of climate cannot be prevented.]*

same, can never be completely warded off, though they may be mitigated by care, and the constant supervision of the soldier; and it is not therefore necessary, I think, for me in this essay to dwell on such points.

Syphilis may be greatly checked by the "Contagious Diseases Act."

I may be equally brief with regard to the prevention of syphilis, to which so much attention has been recently paid; but I take this opportunity to express my unqualified opinion, from practical experience, of the great benefit that has already accrued to the army by the passing of the "Contagious Diseases Act," and my hope that this Act may ere long be extended to the whole civil population, and the disease be thus kept almost completely under control.

With regard to non-inspection, it appears to me highly improbable that a soldier will place himself under the restrictions necessarily attaching to life in hospital until the sore causes him pain or inconvenience, or there is no hope of its unassisted cure.

Soldiers to forfeit pay for concealing their disease.

The forfeiture of pay, however, during residence in hospital for treatment of the *primary* sore in all cases in which the medical officer is of opinion that the disease has for a time been concealed, might operate sufficiently well to relieve the surgeon from a duty which could never be otherwise than most distasteful to him.

The excessive use of stimulants in this

country, and more especially in those of higher temperatures, is another question of great importance in connection with the army, but scarcely one upon which it is necessary here to dilate; nor also upon the minor questions of the prejudicial effect of large doses of quinine on the heart, as suggested by some observers, for this has not as yet been at all proved. *Important to check the abuse of stimulants.*

However difficult or impossible it may be to prevent the diseases of the heart which owe their origin to causes such as the above, that cannot be said of those clearly attributable to the mechanical obstruction to the circulation by the clothing and accoutrements of the soldier, and especially in tropical climates. A most practical proof of this was given by the fatal march of the troops at Chin-Kiang-Foo, and it is quoted by Dr. Maclean in connection with the *cardiac* variety of sunstroke. The 98th Regiment, healthy and strong, having only just landed, and dressed according to regulation, ascended the heights. The heat was intense, and from this form of sunstroke numbers fell down dead by the way; whereas, the 18th, 49th, and 55th Regiments, equally exposed, but with their jackets open and their stocks removed, did not lose a single man from the same cause on that memorable occasion. *Mechanical obstruction easy to remedy.* *The fatal march at Chin-Kiang-Foo.*

To give another illustration. I have shown (*vide* page 18) that in the United Kingdom the

Explanation of Infantry suffering more from heart disease than Cavalry in United Kingdom, and vice versâ in India.

infantry suffer more than the cavalry from heart disease, and that the reverse holds good to a marked extent in India. Now in India, throughout a great part of the year, the infantry soldier wears loose clothing at drills, &c.; whereas, even in undress, the cavalry have to go through their exercises dressed generally in small tight jackets. And I have been told by many men of this arm of the service that they have frequently felt great oppression of the chest and palpitation to arise from riding in the constrained position taught them *without stirrups*, and also from vaulting on and off their horses without the assistance of the same.

Injury of tight clothing has been fully established.

The prejudicial effect of tight clothing and accoutrements has, however, been fully established, and great changes for the better are being rapidly made in them; but, as in the new pattern clothing, though looseness round the chest has been gained, constriction of the neck remains, even after removal of the stock, I would specially urge that this also should be remedied. The following curious anecdote, for which I have to thank Dr. Parkes, is of special interest in connection with the above.

Bèque, in his translation of Donald Morno's work, writes:—

Bèque's anecdote.

"A Danish captain was accustomed to make all the men of his company tie their cravattes very tightly, and use garters very tightly pulled below the knee, so that from the high colour of the face and the size of the calf they might appear more vigorous and better fed; but at the end of a certain time they almost all fell ill."

This peculiar fancy is evidently not yet quite extinct, for I recently heard a private tell his commanding officer that " he liked his collar very tight, because it made his face look red."

The new valise is undoubtedly a great improvement on the knapsack; but I hope the day is not far distant when the soldier will be relieved from carrying his kit, and thus, beyond the great advantage gained to his health, he will be rendered doubly useful—a point of growing importance to the country, as in each succeeding year his value increases, and rapidity of movement becomes more essential to warfare.

Until these changes are actually put in force, much may be done to check the great prevalence of heart disease in the army.

If it is necessary to enlist recruits at the age of eighteen or earlier, it should never be forgotten that they are far from fully developed, and consequently that non-constriction of their vital organs and bones is of the utmost importance to them.

Recruits should not enlist too early.

It would be far better to limit the age to twenty, and in such regiments as the Guards, where the standard is high, this, I am certain, should be imperative.

<small>The training of recruits should not be too severe.</small>

The training of recruits should extend over a longer period, and, like gymnastics, should not be severe at first. I have often seen recruits perfectly exhausted after their morning's drill, and I am led to believe that the course of instruction they undergo is, owing to its severity, particularly obnoxious to them, and it is one, I am sure, that, with the present uniform, is very apt to lay the foundation of much heart disease in the army.

<small>Occupation at first in instructions in trades advocated.</small>

The occupation of the army in various trades is now becoming much advocated, and I would suggest that the first year be spent chiefly in that way, for by considerable personal experience I have found that one of the greatest obstacles to the success of workshops has been the fact that so few men knew anything of the trades to which they professed to belong on enlistment; by this means more time would be allowed for the growth of the body under favourable conditions.

<small>Runningdrill, as at present, questionable.</small>

The present system of running drill appears to me of very questionable benefit. To the young soldier it can do no harm, provided his neck and chest are not constricted, but to older men it may prove very prejudicial, by throwing too great a strain on the heart, and tending to produce hypertrophy of the left ventricle and dilatation of the right, as found in men who have been over-trained.

To gymnastics also, though excellent in principle, the same remarks apply.

On long marches and field-days the upper part of the tunic should be unfastened. Dr. Maclean lays great stress on this point, and concerning the same Dr. Parkes thus writes ("Practical Hygiène," p. 410, &c., 3rd edition): —"When war comes with its rude touch everything which is not useful disappears. What can be easiest borne, what gives the most comfort and the greatest protection, is soon found out. The art of the tailor and the orders of the martinet are alike disregarded, and men instinctively return to what is at the same time most simple and most useful. It will be admitted that the soldier intended for war should be always dressed as if he was to be called upon the next moment to take the field. Everything should be as simple and effective as possible; utility, comfort, durability, and facility of repair are the principles which should regulate all else." . . . " On every account, physiological and mechanical, the neck should be left as bare as possible. Nor is there any reason why it should not be." . . "If the neck is covered at all it

Parkes on clothing.

should be with a very thin and supple cloth. The collar of the coat should be made low and loose, so as to give full freedom to every movement of the neck, and not to compress the root of the neck in the slightest degree. A good tunic should have a low collar, be loose round the neck, over the shoulders, and across the chest."

What clearer statement could I adduce in support of my views! I would only add that as regards men who can grow a beard, Nature has supplied the most efficient means for the protection of the neck, and that I would therefore strongly advocate its general adoption.

In concluding this Essay, I may state my opinion that, when measures such as those above suggested have been adopted, heart disease will gradually diminish in our army, and in time be even less prevalent than in the civil population; and that commanding officers should be made fully aware of the great and permanent injury they may entail on their men, as well as loss they may cause to the service, by their carrying out, so far as they can, their own particular views of what is necessary to make their men look "smart and well set up," and that they should rather bear in mind the motto I have chosen to prefix to this Essay—

"Tempora mutantur nos et mutamur in illis."

THE ALEXANDER MEMORIAL FUND.

TRUSTEES.

Sir James Gibson, K.C.B.
Dr. Mapleton, Inspector-General of Hospitals.
Surgeon-Major Tufnell.

GENERAL COMMITTEE OF OFFICERS IN THE UNITED KINGDOM, 1863.

J. B. Gibson, Esq., C.B., Director-General, Army Medical Department.
Sir Geo. Browne, G C.B., Commander of the Forces in Ireland.
Colonel Whitmore, C.B., Military Sec. in Ireland.
E. J. Parkes, Esq., M.D., Professor of Hygiène.
T. G. Logan, Esq., M.D.
Graham Balfour, Esq., M.D.
Richard Dane, Esq., M.D.
John Frazer, Esq., C.B.
Patrick Gammie, Esq.
Thomas Longmore, Esq.
Henry Mapleton, Esq., M.D.
J. E. T. Parratt, Esq.
George Anderson, Esq., Staff.
J. Davies, Esq., Staff.
Gideon Dolmage, Esq., M.D., Staff.
James C. Dempster, Esq., Staff.
William Home, Esq., M.D., Staff.
E. W. Stone, Esq., M.D., Staff.
D. P. Barry, Esq., Military Train.
Robert Bowen, Esq., Rifle Brigade.
Alexander Browne, Esq., h.p. 23rd Fusiliers.
P. H. E. Cross, Esq., Staff.
J. P. Cunningham, Esq., Staff.
Robt. Cooper, Esq., 4th Drag. Guards.
St. Croix Crosse, Esq., 11th Hussars.
John Coates, Esq., 26th Regt.

John Dunlop, Esq., M.D., Staff.
F. G. Fitzgerald, Esq., Staff.
James Jopp, Esq., M.D., 36th Regt.
A. P. Lockwood, Esq., 2nd Dragoons.
C. W. Poulton, Esq., Staff.
C. R. Robinson, Esq., 25th Regt.
Thomas R. Scott, Esq., Musselburgh.
Benjamin Tydd, Esq., Staff.
Godfrey Watt, Esq., 15th Hussars.
W. Bradshaw, Esq., Staff, V.C.
George Bouchier, Esq., Staff.
C. H. Browne, Esq., 15th Hussars.
J. Clarke, Esq., 95th Regt.
Oliver Codrington, Esq., Staff.
F. De Chaumont, Esq., M.D., Rifle Brigade.
J. B. Cockburn, Esq., M.D., R.A.
Nicholas Ffolliott, Esq., Staff.
D. O. Holle, Esq., Staff.
J. A. Hanbury, Esq., M.B., 45th Reg.
F. G. Kerin, Esq., Roy. Horse Guards.
J. J. Macarthy, Esq., M.D., Staff.
Ormsby B. Miller, Esq., 11th Hussars.
Frederick O'Conner, Esq., Staff.
E. F. O'Leary, Esq., R.A.
J. C. Ovens, Esq., 19th Regt.
J. H. Spry, Esq., Staff.
W. D. Smythe, Esq., Staff.
W. R. Stenart, Esq., R.A.
J. Wood, Esq., R.A.
W. B. Wallis, Esq., R.A.

The General Committee having carried out the original design of a bust of Mr. Alexander, and placed it in the Royal Victoria Hospital, Netley, vested the balance of the subscriptions in the names of Trustees, and convened a general meeting of the subscribers to determine the disposal of the surplus amount.

This meeting appointed an executive committee to carry out such arrangements as they might consider most advisable. This committee was composed as follows:—

Sir J. B. Gibson, K.C.B.	Surgeon-Major Dr. Bostock.
Dr. Logan, C.B., Director-General.	Staff-Surgeon Dr. Crawford.
Dr. Balfour, C.B., Inspector-General.	,, Dr. Fyffe.
Mr. Longmore, C.B., Deputy Inspector-General.	,, Dr. De Chaumont.

It was determined by them—

1. That out of the interest of the amount now invested, a medal to be called the Alexander Medal, and to be of not less value than £5, and a purse containing £50, be awarded, once in every three years, to the executive Medical Officer, on full pay, who shall write the best essay on a subject to be selected by the executive committee, and to be competed for under the following conditions:—

2. The selection of subjects to be confined to—

> Military Medicine.
> ,, Surgery.
> ,, Hygiène.

3. The first subject selected for competition to be announced as soon as possible; and the essays to be completed and despatched by the writers to "The President of the Alexander Memorial Fund Committee, 6, Whitehall Yard," on or before the 31st December, 1869.

4. Each essay to be clearly and legibly written, superscribed with a motto, and accompanied by a sealed envelope similarly superscribed, and containing the name of the writer.

5. The relative merits of the essays to be determined by assessors to be selected by the Executive Committee.

6. The prize to be invariably awarded to the best essay offered, without reference to the number of competitors, provided the writer has complied with the prescribed conditions.

7. The subject for the first competition to be—

> "The etiology and prevalence of diseases of the heart among soldiers, as compared with the civil population of those countries in which they are called upon to serve, and the means of prevention or mitigation,—due regard being had to the conditions in which the soldier is unavoidably placed."

London, New Burlington Street,
April, 1870.

MESSRS. CHURCHILL & SONS'

Publications,

IN

MEDICINE

AND THE VARIOUS BRANCHES OF

NATURAL SCIENCE.

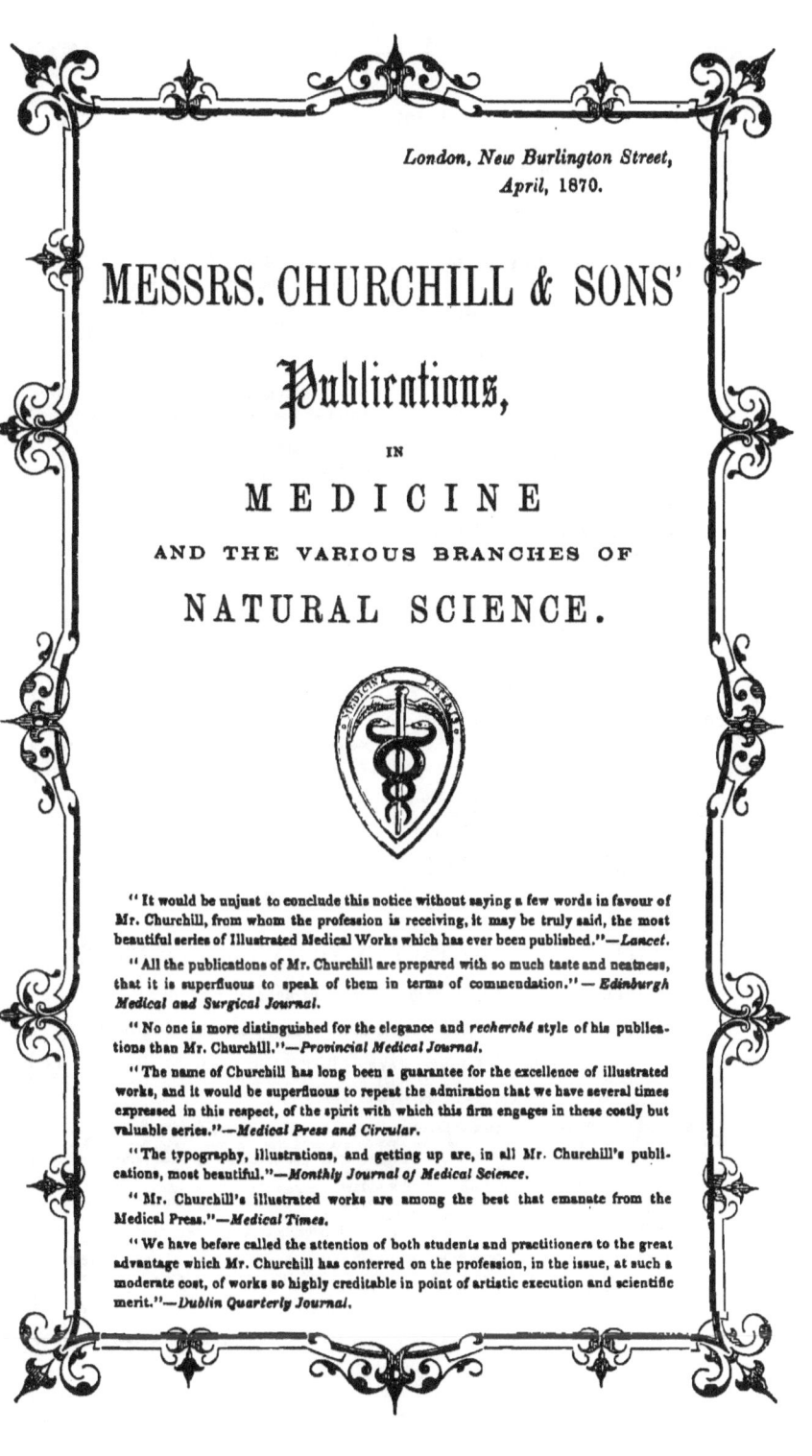

"It would be unjust to conclude this notice without saying a few words in favour of Mr. Churchill, from whom the profession is receiving, it may be truly said, the most beautiful series of Illustrated Medical Works which has ever been published."—*Lancet.*

"All the publications of Mr. Churchill are prepared with so much taste and neatness, that it is superfluous to speak of them in terms of commendation." — *Edinburgh Medical and Surgical Journal.*

"No one is more distinguished for the elegance and *recherché* style of his publications than Mr. Churchill."—*Provincial Medical Journal.*

"The name of Churchill has long been a guarantee for the excellence of illustrated works, and it would be superfluous to repeat the admiration that we have several times expressed in this respect, of the spirit with which this firm engages in these costly but valuable series."—*Medical Press and Circular.*

"The typography, illustrations, and getting up are, in all Mr. Churchill's publications, most beautiful."—*Monthly Journal of Medical Science.*

"Mr. Churchill's illustrated works are among the best that emanate from the Medical Press."—*Medical Times.*

"We have before called the attention of both students and practitioners to the great advantage which Mr. Churchill has conferred on the profession, in the issue, at such a moderate cost, of works so highly creditable in point of artistic execution and scientific merit."—*Dublin Quarterly Journal.*

Messrs. CHURCHILL & SONS are the Publishers of the following Periodicals, offering to Authors a wide extent of Literary Announcement, and a Medium of Advertisement, addressed to all Classes of the Profession.

THE BRITISH AND FOREIGN MEDICO-CHIRURGICAL REVIEW,
AND
QUARTERLY JOURNAL OF PRACTICAL MEDICINE AND SURGERY.
Price Six Shillings. Nos. I. to XC.

THE QUARTERLY JOURNAL OF MICROSCOPICAL SCIENCE,
Edited by Dr. LANKESTER, F.R.S., and E. RAY LANKESTER, B.A., F.R.M.S. Price 4s. Nos. I. to XXXVIII. *New Series.*

THE JOURNAL OF MENTAL SCIENCE.
By authority of the Medico-Psychological Association.
Edited by C. L. ROBERTSON, M.D., and HENRY MAUDSLEY, M.D.
Published Quarterly, price 3s. 6d. *New Series.* Nos. I. to XXXVII.

JOURNAL OF CUTANEOUS MEDICINE.
Edited by ERASMUS WILSON, F.R.S.
Published Quarterly, price 2s. 6d. Nos. I. to XII.

ARCHIVES OF MEDICINE:
A Record of Practical Observations and Anatomical and Chemical Researches, connected with the Investigation and Treatment of Disease. Edited by Dr. LIONEL S. BEALE, F.R.S. Published Quarterly; Nos. I. to VIII., 3s. 6d.; IX. to XII., 2s. 6d., XIII. to XVI., 3s.

THE ROYAL LONDON OPHTHALMIC HOSPITAL REPORTS, AND JOURNAL OF OPHTHALMIC MEDICINE AND SURGERY.
Vol. VI., Part 4, 2s. 6d.

THE MEDICAL TIMES & GAZETTE.
Published Weekly, price Sixpence, or Stamped, Sevenpence.
Annual Subscription, £1. 6s., or Stamped, £1. 10s. 4d., and regularly forwarded to all parts of the Kingdom.

THE PHARMACEUTICAL JOURNAL,
CONTAINING THE TRANSACTIONS OF THE PHARMACEUTICAL SOCIETY.
Published Monthly, price One Shilling.
⁎ Vols. I. to XXVIII., bound in cloth, price 12s. 6d. each.

THE BRITISH JOURNAL OF DENTAL SCIENCE.
Published Monthly, price One Shilling. Nos. I. to CLXVI.

THE MEDICAL DIRECTORY.
Published Annually. 8vo. cloth, 10s. 6d.

THE HALF-YEARLY ABSTRACT OF THE MEDICAL SCIENCES.
BEING A DIGEST OF BRITISH AND CONTINENTAL MEDICINE,
AND OF THE PROGRESS OF MEDICINE AND THE COLLATERAL SCIENCES.

Edited by W. DOMETT STONE, M.D., F.R.C.S., L.S.A.

Post 8vo. cloth, 6s. 6d. Vols. I. to L.

"American physicians may be congratulated that they are once more favoured with the reprint of 'Ranking's Abstract.' If any doctor is so busy that he can read but a single volume a year, then, assuredly, he should make this his book; for here are collected and condensed the most valuable contributions to periodical medical literature—French, German, British, and American—for the year; and, on the other hand, no physician—it matters not how wide the range of his reading—can fail to find, in this volume, truths that will enlarge his medical knowledge, and precepts that will help him in some of his daily professional needs."—*Cincinnati Journal of Medicine,* April, 1867.

"We have only space to say that this volume is rich in valuable articles, among which there are many on materia medica and therapeutics. Gathered from all sources in the new books and medical journals of Europe and America, this work may be viewed as the cream of that class of medical essays, and is a useful occupant of the physician's office-table, to keep him reminded of the progress of medicine."—*American Journal of Pharmacy,* May, 1867.

A CLASSIFIED INDEX
TO
MESSRS. CHURCHILL & SONS' CATALOGUE.

ANATOMY.

	PAGE
Anatomical Remembrancer	7
Flower on Nerves	16
Heale's Anatomy of the Lungs	19
Heath's Practical Anatomy	20
Holden's Human Osteology	20
Do. on Dissections	20
Jones' and Sieveking's Pathological Anatomy	22
MacDougal—Hirschfeld on the Nervous System	v
Maclise's Surgical Anatomy	25
Sibson's Medical Anatomy	33
Waters' Anatomy of Lung	37
Wheeler's Anatomy for Artists	38
Wilson's Anatomy	39

CHEMISTRY.

Bernays' Notes for Students	9
Bloxam's Chemistry	10
Do. Laboratory Teaching	10
Bowman's Practical Chemistry	10
Do. Medical do.	10
Fownes' Manual of Chemistry	16
Do. Actonian Prize	16
Do. Qualitative Analysis	16
Fresenius' Chemical Analysis	17
Galloway's First Step	17
Do. Second Step	17
Do. Analysis	17
Do. Tables	17
Griffiths' Four Seasons	18
Horsley's Chem. Philosophy	21
Kay-Shuttleworth's Modern Chemistry	23
Mulder on the Chemistry of Wine	27
Plattner & Muspratt on Blowpipe	28
Speer's Pathol. Chemistry	34
Sutton's Volumetric Analysis	34

CLIMATE.

Bennet's Winter in the South of Europe	9
Chambers on Italy	12
Dalrymple on Egypt	14
Francis on Change of Climate	16
Grabham on Madeira	18
Hall on Torquay	19
Haviland on Climate	19
Horton on West Coast of Africa	21
Lee on Climate	24
Do. Watering Places of England	24
Martin on Tropical Climates	26
Moore's Diseases of India	26
Patterson's Egypt and the Nile	28
Scoresby-Jackson's Climatology	32
Shapter on South Devon	32
Siordet on Mentone	33
Taylor on Pau and Pyrenees	35

DEFORMITIES, &c.

	PAGE
Adams on Spinal Curvature	6
Do. on Clubfoot	6
Bigg's Orthopraxy	9
Bishop on Deformities	10
Do. Articulate Sounds	10
Brodhurst on Spine	11
Do. on Clubfoot	11
Hugman on Hip Joint	21
Salt on Lower Extremities	31

GENERATIVE ORGANS, Diseases of, and SYPHILIS.

Acton on Reproductive Organs	6
Coote on Syphilis	14
Coulson on Syphilis	14
Gant on Bladder	17
Hutchinson on Inherited Syphilis	22
Lee on Syphilis	23
Oppert on Syphilis	27
Parker on Syphilis	27
Wilson on Syphilis	39

HYGIENE.

Armstrong on Naval Hygiene	7
Beale's Laws of Health	8
Carter on Training	12
Chavasse's Advice to a Mother	13
Do. Counsel to do.	13
Do. Advice to a Wife	13
Dobell's Germs and Vestiges of Disease	15
Fife & Urquhart on Turkish Bath	16
Gordon on Army Hygiene	17
Hartwig on Sea Bathing	19
Hartwig on Physical Education	19
Hufeland's Art of prolonging Life	21
Hunter on Body and Mind	21
Lee's Baths of France, Germany, and Switzerland	24
Lowndes on the Maintenance of Health	25
Moore's Health in Tropics	26
Parkes on Hygiene	28
Parkin on Disease	28
Pearse's Notes on Health	28
Pickford on Hygiene	28
Robertson on Diet	31
Routh on Infant Feeding	31
Wells' Seamen's Medicine Chest	38
Wilson on Healthy Skin	39
Do. on Mineral Waters	39
Do. on Turkish Bath	39

MATERIA MEDICA and PHARMACY.

Beasley's Formulary	9
Do. Receipt Book	9
Do. Book of Prescriptions	9
Birch on Oxygen	9

MATERIA MEDICA and PHARMACY—continued.

	PAGE
Brunton on Digitalis	11
Flux on Sale of Poisons	16
Lescher's Elements of Pharmacy	24
Nevins' Analysis of Pharmacop.	27
Pereira's Selecta è Præscriptis	28
Prescriber's Pharmacopœia	29
Rogers on Therapeutics	31
Royle's Materia Medica	31
Smith's Pharmaceutical Guide	33
Squire's Hospital Pharmacopœias	34
Do. Companion to the Pharmacopœia	34
Steggall's First Lines for Chemists and Druggists	34
Stowe's Toxicological Chart	34
Taylor on Poisons	35
Wahltuch's Materia Medica	37
Waring's Therapeutics	37
Wittstein's Pharmacy	39

MEDICINE.

Adams on Rheumatic Gout	6
Addison on Cell Therapeutics	6
Do. on Healthy and Diseased Structure	6
Aldis's Hospital Practice	6
Anderson (Andrew) on Fever	7
Austin on Paralysis	7
Barclay on Medical Diagnosis	8
Do. on Gout	8
Barlow's Practice of Medicine	8
Basham on Dropsy	8
Braidwood on Pyæmia	10
Brinton on Stomach	11
Do. on Intestinal Obstruction	11
Budd on the Liver	11
Budd on Stomach	11
Camplin on Diabetes	12
Catlow on Æsthetic Medicine	12
Chambers on the Indigestions	12
Do. Lectures	12
Cockle on Cancer	13
Dale's Practical Medicine	14
Davey's Ganglionic Nervous Syst.	14
Day's Clinical Histories	15
Elam on Medicine, Disease, and Death	15
Eyre on Stomach	15
Fenwick on the Stomach	16
Do. on Diagnosis	16
Fuller on Rheumatism	16
Gairdner on Gout	17
Gibb on Throat	17
Do. on Laryngoscope	17
Gully's Simple Treatment	18
Habershon on the Abdomen	18
Do. on Mercury	18
Hall (Marshall) on Apnœa	18
Do. Observations	18
Headland—Action of Medicines	19
Do. Medical Handbook	19
Hooper's Physician's Vade Mecum	18

CLASSIFIED INDEX.

MEDICINE—continued.
	PAGE
Inman's New Theory	22
Do. Myalgia	22
James on Laryngoscope	22
Jencken on Cholera	22
Jones (Bence) on Pathology and Therapeutics	22
Mackenzie on Hoarseness	25
Maclachlan on Advanced Life	25
MacLeod on Acholic Diseases	25
Macleod's Ben Rhydding	25
Macnamara on Cholera	25
Marcet on Chronic Alcoholism	26
Macpherson on Cholera	26
Markham on Bleeding	26
Martyn on Hooping Cough	26
Morris on Germinal Matter	27
Meryon on Paralysis	26
Mushet on Apoplexy	27
Parkin on Cholera	28
Pavy on Diabetes	28
Do. on Digestion	28
Roberts on Palsy	31
Robertson on Gout	31
Sansom on Cholera	32
Savory's Domestic Medicine	32
Semple on Cough	32
Seymour on Dropsy	32
Shaw's Medical Remembrancer	32
Shrimpton on Cholera	32
Smee on Debility	33
Steggall's Medical Manual	34
Thomas' Practice of Physic	35
Thudichum on Gall Stones	35
Todd's Clinical Lectures	36
Tweedie on Continued Fevers	36
Walker on Diphtheria	37
What to Observe at the Bedside	25
Williams' Principles	38
Wright on Headaches	39

MICROSCOPE.
Beale on Microscope in Medicine	8
Carpenter on Microscope	12
Schacht on do.	32

MISCELLANEOUS.
Acton on Prostitution	6
Barclay's Medical Errors	8
Bascome on Epidemics	8
Buckle's Hospital Statistics	11
Cooley's Cyclopædia	13
Edwards' Photographs	15
Gordon on China	17
Graves' Physiology and Medicine	17
Guy's Hospital Reports	17
Harrison on Lead in Water	19
Hingeston's Topics of the Day	20
Howe on Epidemics	21
Lee on Homœop. and Hydrop	24
London Hospital Reports	24
Mayne's Medical Vocabulary	26
Oppert on Hospitals	27
Part's Case Book	28
Redwood's Supplement to Pharmacopœia	30
Ryan on Infanticide	31
St. George's Hospital Reports	31
Simms' Winter in Paris	33
Snow on Chloroform	33
Veitch on Sick Nursing	37
Waring's Tropical Resident at Home	37
Whitehead on Transmission	38
Wise's Med. amongst Asiatics	38

NERVOUS DISORDERS AND INDIGESTION.
	PAGE
Althaus on Epilepsy, Hysteria, &c.	7
Birch on Constipation	9
Downing on Neuralgia	15
Hunt on Heartburn	21
Jones (Handfield) on Functional Nervous Disorders	22
Leared on Imperfect Digestion	23
Morris on Irritability	26
Reade on Syphilitic Affections of the Nervous System	30
Reynolds on the Brain	30
Do. on Epilepsy	30
Rowe on Nervous Diseases	31
Sieveking on Epilepsy	33
Turnbull on Stomach	36

OBSTETRICS.
Barnes on Obstetric Operations	8
Hodges on Puerperal Convulsions	20
Lee's Clinical Midwifery	24
Do. Consultations	24
Leishman's Mechanism of Parturition	24
Pretty's Aids during Labour	29
Priestley on Gravid Uterus	30
Ramsbotham's Obstetrics	30
Sinclair & Johnston's Midwifery	33
Smellie's Obstetric Plates	33
Smith's Manual of Obstetrics	33
Swayne's Aphorisms	34
Waller's Midwifery	37

OPHTHALMOLOGY.
Cooper on Injuries of Eye	13
Do. on Near Sight	13
Dalrymple on Eye	14
Dixon on the Eye	15
Hogg on Ophthalmoscope	20
Hulke on the Ophthalmoscope	21
Jago on Entoptics	22
Jones' Ophthalmic Medicine	23
Do. Defects of Sight	23
Do. Eye and Ear	23
Macnamara on the Eye	25
Nunneley on the Organs of Vision	27
Power's Illustrations of Diseases of the Eye	29
Solomon on Glaucoma	34
Walton on the Eye	37
Wells Treatise on the Eye	38
Do. on Spectacles	38
Wolfe on Cataract	39

PHYSIOLOGY.
Beale on Protoplasm	8
Carpenter's Human	12
Do. Manual	12
Heale on Vital Causes	19
Richardson on Coagulation	30
Shea's Animal Physiology	32

PSYCHOLOGY.
	PAGE
Arlidge on the State of Lunacy	7
Bucknill and Tuke's Psychological Medicine	11
Davey on Nature of Insanity	14
Hood on Criminal Lunatics	21
Murray on Emotional Diseases	27
Noble on Mind	27
Sankey on Mental Diseases	31
Van der Kolk on Mental Disease	37
Winslow's Obscure Dis. of Brain	39

PULMONARY and CHEST DISEASES, &c.
Alison on Pulmonary Consumption	6
Bright on the Chest	10
Cotton on Stethoscope	14
Davies on Lungs and Heart	14
Dobell on the Chest	15
Do. on Tuberculosis	15
Do. on Winter Cough	15
Do. First Stage of Consumption	15
Fuller on the Lungs	16
Do. on Heart	16
Jones (Jas.) on Consumption	23
Laennec on Auscultation	23
Markham on Heart	26
Peacock on the Heart	28
Pirrie on Hay Asthma	29
Salter on Asthma	31
Skoda on Auscultation	26
Thompson on Consumption	35
Thorowgood on Asthma	35
Timms on Consumption	36
Turnbull on Consumption	36
Waters on the Chest	37
Do. on Emphysema	37

RENAL and URINARY DISEASES.
Acton on Urinary Organs	6
Basham on Renal Diseases	8
Beale on Kidney Diseases	8
Bird's Urinary Deposits	10
Coulson on Bladder	14
Hassall on Urine	19
Parkes on Urine	28
Thudichum on Urine	35
Todd on Urinary Organs	36

SCIENCE.
Baxter on Organic Polarity	8
Bentley's Manual of Botany	9
Brooke's Natural Philosophy	11
Hardwich's Photography	19
Hinds' Harmonies	20
Howard on the Clouds	21
Huxley on Classification of Animals	22
Jones (Bence) on Matter and Force	22
Jones (Wharton) on Vision	23
Do. on Body, Sense, and Mind	23
Mayne's Lexicon of Terms	26
Noad on the Inductorium	27

CLASSIFIED INDEX.

SCIENCE—continued.	PAGE
Pratt's Genealogy of Creation	29
Do. Eccentric & Centric Force	29
Do. on Orbital Motion	29
Do. Astronomical Investigations	29
Do. Oracles of God	29
Price's Photography	30
Rainey on Shells	30
Reymond's Animal Electricity	30
Taylor's Medical Jurisprudence	35
Vestiges of Creation	36

SURGERY.	PAGE
Adams on Reparation of Tendons	6
Do. Subcutaneous Surgery	6
Anderson on the Skin	7
Ashton on Rectum	7
Brodhurst on Anchylosis	11
Bryant on Diseases of Joints	11
Do. Clinical Surgery	11
Callender on Rupture	12
Chapman on Ulcers	12
Do. Varicose Veins	12
Clark on Visceral Lesions	13
Do. Outlines of Surgery	13
Collis on Cancer	13
Cooper's Surgical Dictionary	14
Coulson on Stone in Bladder	14
Curling on Rectum	14
Do. on Testis	14
Druitt's Surgeon's Vade-Mecum	15
Fayrer's Clinical Surgery	15
Fergusson's Surgery	16
Do. Progress of Surgery	16
Gamgee's Amputation at Hip-joint	17
Gant's Principles of Surgery	17

SURGERY—continued.	PAGE
Gay on Varicose Disease	17
Heath's Minor Surgery and Bandaging	20
Do. on the Jaws	20
Higginbottom on Nitrate of Silver	20
Hodgson on Prostate	20
Holt on Stricture	21
Lawrence's Surgery	23
Do. Ruptures	23
Lee's Practical Pathology	23
Liston's Surgery	24
Logan on Skin Diseases	24
Macleod's Surgical Diagnosis	25
Macleod's Surgery of the Crimea	25
Maclise on Fractures	25
Marsden on Cancer	26
Maunder's Operative Surgery	26
Nayler on Skin Diseases	27
Nunneley on Erysipelas	27
Pirrie's Surgery	29
Price on Excision of Knee-joint	29
Ramsay and Coles on Deformities of the Mouth	30
Sansom on Chloroform	32
Smith (Hy.) on Stricture	33
Do. on Hæmorrhoids	33
Do. on the Surgery of the Rectum	33
Do. (Dr. J.) Dental Anatomy and Surgery	33
Spender on Ulcers	34
Steggall's Surgical Manual	34
Swain on the Knee-Joint	34
Thompson on Stricture	35
Do. on Prostate	35
Do. Lithotomy and Lithotrity	35
Do. on Urinary Organs	35
Tomes' Dental Surgery	36
Wade on Stricture	37

SURGERY—continued.	PAGE
Webb's Surgeon's Ready Rules	38
Wilson on Skin Diseases	39
Do. Portraits of Skin Diseases	39

VETERINARY MEDICINE.	PAGE
Blaine's Veterinary Art	10
Bourguignon on the Cattle Plague	10
Haycock on Shoeing Horses	19
Tuson's Pharmacopœia	36

WOMEN AND CHILDREN, Diseases of.	PAGE
Ballard on Infants and Mothers	7
Bennet on Uterus	9
Ellis on Children	15
Eyre's Practical Remarks	15
Harrison on Children	19
Hood on Scarlet Fever, &c.	21
Kiwisch (ed. by Clay) on Ovaries	13
Lee's Ovarian & Uterine Diseases	24
Do. on Speculum	24
Norton on Infantile Diseases	27
Seymour on Ovaria	32
Tilt on Uterine Inflammation	36
Do. Uterine Therapeutics	36
Do. on Change of Life	36
Underwood on Children	36
West on Women	38
Wright on Uterine Disorders	39

TO BE COMPLETED IN TWELVE PARTS, 4TO., AT 7s. 6d. PER PART.

PARTS I. & II. NOW READY.

A DESCRIPTIVE TREATISE
ON THE
NERVOUS SYSTEM OF MAN,
WITH THE MANNER OF DISSECTING IT.

BY LUDOVIC HIRSCHFELD,

DOCTOR OF MEDICINE OF THE UNIVERSITIES OF PARIS AND WARSAW, PROFESSOR OF ANATOMY TO THE FACULTY OF MEDICINE OF WARSAW;

Edited in English (from the French Edition of 1866)

BY ALEXANDER MASON MACDOUGAL, F.R.C.S.,

WITH

AN ATLAS OF ARTISTICALLY-COLOURED ILLUSTRATIONS,

Embracing the Anatomy of the entire Cerebro-Spinal and Sympathetic Nervous Centres and Distributions in their accurate relations with all the important Constituent Parts of the Human Economy, and embodied in a series of 56 Single and 9 Double Plates, comprising 197 Illustrations,

Designed from Dissections prepared by the Author, and Drawn on Stone by
J. B. LÉVEILLÉ.

WILLIAM ACTON, M.R.C.S.

I.
A PRACTICAL TREATISE ON DISEASES OF THE URINARY AND GENERATIVE ORGANS IN BOTH SEXES. Third Edition. 8vo. cloth, £1. 1s. With Plates, £1. 11s. 6d. The Plates alone, limp cloth, 10s. 6d.

II.
THE FUNCTIONS AND DISORDERS OF THE REPRODUC-TIVE ORGANS IN CHILDHOOD, YOUTH, ADULT AGE, AND ADVANCED LIFE, considered in their Physiological, Social, and Moral Relations. Fourth Edition. 8vo. cloth, 10s. 6d.

III.
PROSTITUTION: Considered in its Moral, Social, and Sanitary Aspects, Second Edition, enlarged. 8vo. cloth, 12s.

ROBERT ADAMS, A.M., C.M., M.D.

A TREATISE ON RHEUMATIC GOUT; OR, CHRONIC RHEUMATIC ARTHRITIS. 8vo. cloth, with a Quarto Atlas of Plates, 21s.

WILLIAM ADAMS, F.R.C.S.

I.
ON THE PATHOLOGY AND TREATMENT OF LATERAL AND OTHER FORMS OF CURVATURE OF THE SPINE. With Plates. 8vo. cloth, 10s. 6d.

II.
CLUBFOOT: its Causes, Pathology, and Treatment. Jacksonian Prize Essay for 1864. With 100 Engravings. 8vo. cloth, 12s.

III.
ON THE REPARATIVE PROCESS IN HUMAN TENDONS AFTER SUBCUTANEOUS DIVISION FOR THE CURE OF DEFORMITIES. With Plates. 8vo. cloth, 6s.

IV.
SKETCH OF THE PRINCIPLES AND PRACTICE OF SUBCUTANEOUS SURGERY. 8vo. cloth, 2s. 6d.

WILLIAM ADDISON, F.R.C.P., F.R.S.

I.
CELL THERAPEUTICS. 8vo. cloth, 4s.

II.
ON HEALTHY AND DISEASED STRUCTURE, AND THE TRUE PRINCIPLES OF TREATMENT FOR THE CURE OF DISEASE, ESPECIALLY CONSUMPTION AND SCROFULA, founded on MICROSCOPICAL ANALYSIS. 8vo. cloth, 12s.

C. J. B. ALDIS, M.D., F.R.C.P.

AN INTRODUCTION TO HOSPITAL PRACTICE IN VARIOUS COMPLAINTS; with Remarks on their Pathology and Treatment. 8vo. cloth, 5s. 6d.

SOMERVILLE SCOTT ALISON, M.D.EDIN., F.R.C.P.

THE PHYSICAL EXAMINATION OF THE CHEST IN PUL-MONARY CONSUMPTION, AND ITS INTERCURRENT DISEASES. With Engravings. 8vo. cloth, 12s.

JULIUS ALTHAUS, M.D., M.R.C.P.
ON EPILEPSY, HYSTERIA, AND ATAXY. Cr. 8vo. cloth, 4s.

THE ANATOMICAL REMEMBRANCER; OR, COMPLETE POCKET ANATOMIST. Sixth Edition, carefully Revised. 32mo. cloth, 3s. 6d.

McCALL ANDERSON, M.D., F.F.P.S.
I.
THE PARASITIC AFFECTIONS OF THE SKIN. Second Edition. With Engravings. 8vo. cloth, 7s. 6d.

II.
ECZEMA. Second Edition. 8vo. cloth, 6s.

III.
PSORIASIS AND LEPRA. With Chromo-lithograph. 8vo. cloth, 5s.

ANDREW ANDERSON, M.D.
TEN LECTURES INTRODUCTORY TO THE STUDY OF FEVER. Post 8vo. cloth, 5s.

J. T. ARLIDGE, M.D.LOND., F.R.C.P.
ON THE STATE OF LUNACY AND THE LEGAL PROVISION FOR THE INSANE; with Observations on the Construction and Organisation of Asylums. 8vo. cloth, 7s.

ALEXANDER ARMSTRONG, M.D., F.R.C.P., R.N.
OBSERVATIONS ON NAVAL HYGIENE AND SCURVY. More particularly as the latter appeared during a Polar Voyage. 8vo. cloth, 5s.

T. J. ASHTON, M.R.C.S.
I.
ON THE DISEASES, INJURIES, AND MALFORMATIONS OF THE RECTUM AND ANUS. Fourth Edition. 8vo. cloth, 8s.

II.
PROLAPSUS, FISTULA IN ANO, AND OTHER DISEASES OF THE RECTUM; their Pathology and Treatment. Third Edition. Post 8vo. cloth, 3s. 6d.

THOS. J. AUSTIN, M.R.C.S.ENG.
A PRACTICAL ACCOUNT OF GENERAL PARALYSIS; Its Mental and Physical Symptoms, Statistics, Causes, Seat, and Treatment. 8vo. cloth, 6s.

THOMAS BALLARD, M.D.
A NEW AND RATIONAL EXPLANATION OF THE DISEASES PECULIAR TO INFANTS AND MOTHERS; with obvious Suggestions for their Prevention and Cure. Post 8vo. cloth, 4s. 6d.

MESSRS. CHURCHILL & SONS' PUBLICATIONS.

A. W. BARCLAY, M.D., F.R.C.P.

I.
A MANUAL OF MEDICAL DIAGNOSIS. Second Edition.
Foolscap 8vo. cloth, 8s. 6d.

II.
MEDICAL ERRORS.—Fallacies connected with the Application of the Inductive Method of Reasoning to the Science of Medicine. Post 8vo. cloth, 5s.

III.
GOUT AND RHEUMATISM IN RELATION TO DISEASE OF THE HEART. Post 8vo. cloth, 5s.

G. H. BARLOW, M.D., F.R.C.P.

A MANUAL OF THE PRACTICE OF MEDICINE. Second Edition. Fcap. 8vo. cloth, 12s. 6d.

ROBERT BARNES, M.D., F.R.C.P.

LECTURES ON OBSTETRIC OPERATIONS, INCLUDING THE TREATMENT OF HÆMORRHAGE, and forming a Guide to the Management of Difficult Labour. With nearly 100 Engravings. 8vo. cloth, 15s.

E. BASCOME, M.D.

A HISTORY OF EPIDEMIC PESTILENCES, FROM THE EARLIEST AGES. 8vo. cloth, 8s.

W. R. BASHAM, M.D., F.R.C.P.

I.
RENAL DISEASES; a CLINICAL GUIDE to their DIAGNOSIS and TREATMENT. 8vo. cloth, 7s.

II.
ON DROPSY, AND ITS CONNECTION WITH DISEASES OF THE KIDNEYS, HEART, LUNGS AND LIVER. With 16 Plates. Third Edition. 8vo. cloth, 12s. 6d.

H. F. BAXTER, M.R.C.S.L.

ON ORGANIC POLARITY; showing a Connexion to exist between Organic Forces and Ordinary Polar Forces. Crown 8vo. cloth, 5s.

LIONEL J. BEALE, M.R.C.S.

THE LAWS OF HEALTH IN THEIR RELATIONS TO MIND AND BODY. A Series of Letters from an Old Practitioner to a Patient. Post 8vo. cloth, 7s. 6d.

LIONEL S. BEALE, M.B., F.R.S., F.R.C.P.

I.
ON KIDNEY DISEASES, URINARY DEPOSITS, AND CALCULOUS DISORDERS. Third Edition, much Enlarged. With 70 Plates. 8vo. cloth, 25s.

II.
THE MICROSCOPE, IN ITS APPLICATION TO PRACTICAL MEDICINE. Third Edition. With 58 Plates. 8vo. cloth, 16s.

III.
PROTOPLASM; OR, LIFE, MATTER AND MIND. Second Edition. With 8 Plates. Crown 8vo. cloth, 6s. 6d.

MESSRS. CHURCHILL & SONS' PUBLICATIONS. 9

HENRY BEASLEY.

I.
THE BOOK OF PRESCRIPTIONS; containing 3000 Prescriptions. Collected from the Practice of the most eminent Physicians and Surgeons, English and Foreign. Third Edition. 18mo. cloth, 6s.

II.
THE DRUGGIST'S GENERAL RECEIPT-BOOK: comprising a copious Veterinary Formulary and Table of Veterinary Materia Medica; Patent and Proprietary Medicines, Druggists' Nostrums, &c.; Perfumery, Skin Cosmetics, Hair Cosmetics, and Teeth Cosmetics; Beverages, Dietetic Articles, and Condiments; Trade Chemicals, Miscellaneous Preparations and Compounds used in the Arts, &c.; with useful Memoranda and Tables. Sixth Edition. 18mo. cloth, 6s.

III.
THE POCKET FORMULARY AND SYNOPSIS OF THE BRITISH AND FOREIGN PHARMACOPŒIAS; comprising standard and approved Formulæ for the Preparations and Compounds employed in Medical Practice. Eighth Edition, corrected and enlarged. 18mo. cloth, 6s.

HENRY BENNET, M.D.

I.
A PRACTICAL TREATISE ON UTERINE DISEASES. Fourth Edition, revised, with Additions. 8vo. cloth, 16s.

II.
WINTER AND SPRING ON THE SHORES OF THE MEDITERRANEAN: OR, THE RIVIERA, MENTONE, ITALY, CORSICA, SICILY, ALGERIA, SPAIN, AND BIARRITZ, AS WINTER CLIMATES. Fourth Edition, with numerous Plates, Maps, and Wood Engravings. Post 8vo. cloth, 12s.

ROBERT BENTLEY, F.L.S.

A MANUAL OF BOTANY. With nearly 1,200 Engravings on Wood. Fcap. 8vo. cloth, 12s. 6d.

ALBERT J. BERNAYS, PH.D., F.C.S.

NOTES FOR STUDENTS IN CHEMISTRY; being a Syllabus compiled from the Manuals of Miller, Fownes, Berzelius, Gerhardt, Gorup-Besanez, &c. Fifth Edition. Fcap. 8vo. cloth, 3s. 6d.

HENRY HEATHER BIGG.

ORTHOPRAXY: a complete Guide to the Modern Treatment of Deformities by Mechanical Appliances. With 300 Engravings. Second Edition. Post 8vo. cloth, 10s.

S. B. BIRCH M.D., M.R.C.P.

I.
OXYGEN: ITS ACTION, USE, AND VALUE IN THE TREATMENT OF VARIOUS DISEASES OTHERWISE INCURABLE OR VERY INTRACTABLE. Second Edition. Post 8vo. cloth, 3s. 6d.

II.
CONSTIPATED BOWELS: the Various Causes and the Different Means of Cure. Third Edition. Post 8vo. cloth, 3s. 6d.

GOLDING BIRD, M.D., F.R.S.

URINARY DEPOSITS; THEIR DIAGNOSIS, PATHOLOGY, AND THERAPEUTICAL INDICATIONS. With Engravings. Fifth Edition. Edited by E. LLOYD BIRKETT, M.D. Post 8vo. cloth, 10s. 6d.

JOHN BISHOP, F.R.C.S., F.R.S.

I.
ON DEFORMITIES OF THE HUMAN BODY, their Pathology and Treatment. With Engravings on Wood. 8vo. cloth, 10s.

II.
ON ARTICULATE SOUNDS, AND ON THE CAUSES AND CURE OF IMPEDIMENTS OF SPEECH. 8vo. cloth, 4s.

BLAINE.

OUTLINES OF THE VETERINARY ART; OR, A TREATISE ON THE ANATOMY, PHYSIOLOGY, AND DISEASES OF THE HORSE, NEAT CATTLE, AND SHEEP. Seventh Edition. By Charles Steel, M.R.C.V.S.L. With Plates. 8vo. cloth, 18s.

O. L. BLOXAM.

I.
CHEMISTRY, INORGANIC AND ORGANIC; with Experiments and a Comparison of Equivalent and Molecular Formulæ. With 276 Engravings on Wood. 8vo. cloth, 16s.

II.
LABORATORY TEACHING; OR PROGRESSIVE EXERCISES IN PRACTICAL CHEMISTRY. With 89 Engravings. Crown, 8vo. cloth, 5s. 6d.

HONORÉ BOURGUIGNON, M.D.

ON THE CATTLE PLAGUE; OR, CONTAGIOUS TYPHUS IN HORNED CATTLE: its History, Origin, Description, and Treatment. Post 8vo. 5s.

JOHN E. BOWMAN, & O. L. BLOXAM.

I.
PRACTICAL CHEMISTRY, including Analysis. With numerous Illustrations on Wood. Fifth Edition. Foolscap 8vo. cloth, 6s. 6d.

II.
MEDICAL CHEMISTRY; with Illustrations on Wood. Fourth Edition, carefully revised. Fcap. 8vo. cloth, 6s. 6d.

P. MURRAY BRAIDWOOD, M.D. EDIN.

ON PYÆMIA, OR SUPPURATIVE FEVER: the Astley Cooper Prize Essay for 1868. With 12 Plates. 8vo. cloth, 10s. 6d.

JAMES BRIGHT, M.D.

ON DISEASES OF THE HEART, LUNGS, & AIR PASSAGES; with a Review of the several Climates recommended in these Affections. Third Edition. Post 8vo. cloth, 9s.

WILLIAM BRINTON, M.D., F.R.S.

I.
THE DISEASES OF THE STOMACH, with an Introduction on its Anatomy and Physiology; being Lectures delivered at St. Thomas's Hospital. Second Edition. 8vo. cloth, 10s. 6d.

II.
INTESTINAL OBSTRUCTION. Edited by Dr. Buzzard. Post 8vo. cloth, 5s.

BERNARD E. BRODHURST, F.R.C.S.

I.
CURVATURES OF THE SPINE: their Causes, Symptoms, Pathology, and Treatment. Second Edition. Roy. 8vo. cloth, with Engravings, 7s. 6d.

II.
ON THE NATURE AND TREATMENT OF CLUBFOOT AND ANALOGOUS DISTORTIONS involving the TIBIO-TARSAL ARTICULATION. With Engravings on Wood. 8vo. cloth, 4s. 6d.

III.
PRACTICAL OBSERVATIONS ON THE DISEASES OF THE JOINTS INVOLVING ANCHYLOSIS, and on the TREATMENT for the RESTORATION of MOTION. Third Edition, much enlarged, 8vo. cloth, 4s. 6d.

CHARLES BROOKE, M.A., M.B., F.R.S.

ELEMENTS OF NATURAL PHILOSOPHY. Based on the Work of the late Dr. Golding Bird. Sixth Edition. With 700 Engravings. Fcap. 8vo. cloth, 12s. 6d.

T. L. BRUNTON, B.SC., M.B.

ON DIGITALIS. With some Observations on the Urine. Fcap. 8vo. cloth, 4s. 6d.

THOMAS BRYANT, F.R.C.S.

I.
ON THE DISEASES AND INJURIES OF THE JOINTS. CLINICAL AND PATHOLOGICAL OBSERVATIONS. Post 8vo. cloth, 7s. 6d.

II.
CLINICAL SURGERY. Parts I. to VII. 8vo., 3s. 6d. each.

FLEETWOOD BUCKLE, M.D., L.R.C.P.LOND.

VITAL AND ECONOMICAL STATISTICS OF THE HOSPITALS, INFIRMARIES, &c., OF ENGLAND AND WALES. Royal 8vo. 5s.

JOHN CHARLES BUCKNILL, M.D., F.R.C.P., F.R.S., & DANIEL H. TUKE, M.D.

A MANUAL OF PSYCHOLOGICAL MEDICINE: containing the History, Nosology, Description, Statistics, Diagnosis, Pathology, and Treatment of Insanity. Second Edition. 8vo. cloth, 15s.

GEORGE BUDD, M.D., F.R.C.P., F.R.S.

I.
ON DISEASES OF THE LIVER. Illustrated with Coloured Plates and Engravings on Wood. Third Edition. 8vo. cloth, 16s.

II.
ON THE ORGANIC DISEASES AND FUNCTIONAL DIS- ORDERS OF THE STOMACH. 8vo. cloth, 9s.

G. W. CALLENDER, F.R.C.S.
FEMORAL RUPTURE: Anatomy of the Parts concerned. With Plates. 8vo. cloth, 4s.

JOHN M. CAMPLIN, M.D., F.L.S.
ON DIABETES, AND ITS SUCCESSFUL TREATMENT. Third Edition, by Dr. Glover. Fcap. 8vo. cloth, 3s. 6d.

ROBERT B. CARTER, F.R.C.S.
ON THE INFLUENCE OF EDUCATION AND TRAINING IN PREVENTING DISEASES OF THE NERVOUS SYSTEM. Fcap. 8vo., 6s.

W. B. CARPENTER, M.D., F.R.S.
I.
PRINCIPLES OF HUMAN PHYSIOLOGY. With nearly 300 Illustrations on Steel and Wood. Seventh Edition. Edited by Mr. Henry Power. 8vo. cloth, 28s.

II.
A MANUAL OF PHYSIOLOGY. With 252 Illustrations on Steel and Wood. Fourth Edition. Fcap. 8vo. cloth, 12s. 6d.

III.
THE MICROSCOPE AND ITS REVELATIONS. With more than 400 Engravings on Steel and Wood. Fourth Edition. Fcap. 8vo. cloth, 12s. 6d.

JOSEPH PEEL CATLOW, M.R.C.S.
ON THE PRINCIPLES OF ÆSTHETIC MEDICINE; or the Natural Use of Sensation and Desire in the Maintenance of Health and the Treatment of Disease. 8vo. cloth, 9s.

T. K. CHAMBERS, M.D., F.R.C.P.
I.
LECTURES, CHIEFLY CLINICAL. Fourth Edition. 8vo. cloth, 14s.

II.
THE INDIGESTIONS OR DISEASES OF THE DIGESTIVE ORGANS FUNCTIONALLY TREATED. Second Edition. 8vo. cloth, 10s. 6d.

III.
SOME OF THE EFFECTS OF THE CLIMATE OF ITALY. Crown 8vo. cloth, 4s. 6d.

H. T. CHAPMAN, F.R.C.S.
I.
THE TREATMENT OF OBSTINATE ULCERS AND CUTANEOUS ERUPTIONS OF THE LEG WITHOUT CONFINEMENT. Third Edition. Post 8vo. cloth, 3s. 6d.

II.
VARICOSE VEINS: their Nature, Consequences, and Treatment, Palliative and Curative. Second Edition. Post 8vo. cloth, 3s. 6d.

PYE HENRY CHAVASSE, F.R.C.S.

I.
ADVICE TO A MOTHER ON THE MANAGEMENT OF HER CHILDREN. Tenth Edition. Foolscap 8vo., 2s. 6d.

II.
COUNSEL TO A MOTHER: being a Continuation and the Completion of "Advice to a Mother." Fcap. 8vo. 2s. 6d.

III.
ADVICE TO A WIFE ON THE MANAGEMENT OF HER OWN HEALTH. With an Introductory Chapter, especially addressed to a Young Wife. Ninth Edition. Fcap. 8vo., 2s. 6d.

F. LE GROS CLARK, F.R.C.S.

I.
LECTURES ON THE PRINCIPLES OF SURGICAL DIAGNOSIS: ESPECIALLY IN RELATION TO SHOCK AND VISCERAL LESIONS Delivered at the Royal College of Surgeons. 8vo. cloth, 10s. 6d.

II.
OUTLINES OF SURGERY; being an Epitome of the Lectures on the Principles and the Practice of Surgery delivered at St. Thomas's Hospital. Fcap. 8vo. cloth, 5s.

JOHN CLAY, M.R.C.S.

KIWISCH ON DISEASES OF THE OVARIES: Translated, by permission, from the last German Edition of his Clinical Lectures on the Special Pathology and Treatment of the Diseases of Women. With Notes, and an Appendix on the Operation of Ovariotomy. Royal 12mo. cloth, 16s.

JOHN COCKLE, M.D., F.R.C.P.

ON INTRA-THORACIC CANCER. 8vo. 6s. 6d.

MAURICE H. COLLIS, M.D.DUB., F.R.C.S.I.

THE DIAGNOSIS AND TREATMENT OF CANCER AND THE TUMOURS ANALOGOUS TO IT. With coloured Plates. 8vo. cloth, 14s.

A. J. COOLEY.

THE CYCLOPÆDIA OF PRACTICAL RECEIPTS, PROCESSES, AND COLLATERAL INFORMATION IN THE ARTS, MANUFACTURES, PROFESSIONS, AND TRADES, INCLUDING MEDICINE, PHARMACY, AND DOMESTIC ECONOMY; designed as a General Book of Reference for the Manufacturer, Tradesman, Amateur, and Heads of Families. Fourth and greatly enlarged Edition, 8vo. cloth, 28s.

W. WHITE COOPER, F.R.C.S.

I.
ON WOUNDS AND INJURIES OF THE EYE. Illustrated by 17 Coloured Figures and 41 Woodcuts. 8vo. cloth, 12s.

II.
ON NEAR SIGHT, AGED SIGHT, IMPAIRED VISION, AND THE MEANS OF ASSISTING SIGHT. With 31 Illustrations on Wood. Second Edition. Fcap. 8vo. cloth, 7s. 6d.

MESSRS. CHURCHILL & SONS' PUBLICATIONS.

S. COOPER.
A DICTIONARY OF PRACTICAL SURGERY AND ENCYCLO-
PÆDIA OF SURGICAL SCIENCE. New Edition, brought down to the present
time. By SAMUEL A. LANE, F.R.C.S., assisted by various eminent Surgeons. Vol. I.,
8vo. cloth, £1. 5s.

HOLMES COOTE, F.R.C.S.
A REPORT ON SOME IMPORTANT POINTS IN THE
TREATMENT OF SYPHILIS. 8vo. cloth, 5s.

R. P. COTTON, M.D., F.R.C.P.
PHTHISIS AND THE STETHOSCOPE; OR, THE PHYSICAL
SIGNS OF CONSUMPTION. Fourth Edition. Foolscap 8vo. cloth, 3s. 6d.

WILLIAM COULSON, F.R.C.S.
ON DISEASES OF THE BLADDER AND PROSTATE GLAND.
New Edition, revised. *In Preparation.*

WALTER J. COULSON, F.R.C.S.
I.
A TREATISE ON SYPHILIS. 8vo. cloth, 10s.
II.
STONE IN THE BLADDER: Its Prevention, Early Symptoms, and
Treatment by Lithotrity. 8vo. cloth, 6s.

T. B. CURLING, F.R.C.S., F.R.S.
I.
OBSERVATIONS ON DISEASES OF THE RECTUM. Third
Edition. 8vo. cloth, 7s. 6d.
II.
A PRACTICAL TREATISE ON DISEASES OF THE TESTIS,
SPERMATIC CORD, AND SCROTUM. Third Edition, with Engravings. 8vo.
cloth, 16s.

WILLIAM DALE, M.D.LOND.
A COMPENDIUM OF PRACTICAL MEDICINE AND MORBID
ANATOMY. With Plates, 12mo. cloth, 7s.

DONALD DALRYMPLE, M.P., M.R.C.P.
THE CLIMATE OF EGYPT: METEOROLOGICAL AND MEDI-
CAL OBSERVATIONS, with Practical Hints for Invalid Travellers. Post 8vo. cloth, 4s.

JOHN DALRYMPLE, F.R.C.S., F.R.S.
PATHOLOGY OF THE HUMAN EYE. Complete in Nine Fasciculi:
imperial 4to., 20s. each; half-bound morocco, gilt tops, 9l. 15s.

HERBERT DAVIES, M.D., F.R.C.P.
ON THE PHYSICAL DIAGNOSIS OF DISEASES OF THE
LUNGS AND HEART. Second Edition. Post 8vo. cloth, 8s.

JAMES G. DAVEY, M.D., M.R.C.P.
I.
THE GANGLIONIC NERVOUS SYSTEM: its Structure, Functions,
and Diseases. 8vo. cloth, 9s.
II.
ON THE NATURE AND PROXIMATE CAUSE OF IN-
SANITY. Post 8vo. cloth, 3s.

HENRY DAY, M.D., M.R.C.P.
CLINICAL HISTORIES; with Comments. 8vo. cloth, 7s. 6d.

JAMES DIXON, F.R.C.S.
A GUIDE TO THE PRACTICAL STUDY OF DISEASES OF THE EYE. Third Edition. Post 8vo. cloth, 9s.

HORACE DOBELL, M.D.

I.
DEMONSTRATIONS OF DISEASES IN THE CHEST, AND THEIR PHYSICAL DIAGNOSIS. With Coloured Plates. 8vo. cloth, 12s. 6d.

II.
LECTURES ON THE GERMS AND VESTIGES OF DISEASE, and on the Prevention of the Invasion and Fatality of Disease by Periodical Examinations. 8vo. cloth, 6s. 6d.

III.
ON TUBERCULOSIS: ITS NATURE, CAUSE, AND TREATMENT; with Notes on Pancreatic Juice. Second Edition. Crown 8vo. cloth, 3s. 6d.

IV.
LECTURES ON WINTER COUGH (CATARRH, BRONCHITIS, EMPHYSEMA, ASTHMA); with an Appendix on some Principles of Diet in Disease. Post 8vo. cloth, 5s. 6d.

V.
LECTURES ON THE TRUE FIRST STAGE OF CONSUMPTION. Crown 8vo. cloth, 3s. 6d.

C. TOOGOOD DOWNING, M.D.
NEURALGIA: its various Forms, Pathology, and Treatment. THE JACKSONIAN PRIZE ESSAY FOR 1850. 8vo. cloth, 10s. 6d.

ROBERT DRUITT, F.R.C.S.
THE SURGEON'S VADE-MECUM; with numerous Engravings on Wood. Ninth Edition. Foolscap 8vo. cloth, 12s. 6d.

ERNEST EDWARDS, B.A.
PHOTOGRAPHS OF EMINENT MEDICAL MEN, with brief Analytical Notices of their Works. Vols. I. and II. (24 Portraits), 4to. cloth, 24s. each.

CHARLES ELAM, M.D., M.R.C.P.
MEDICINE, DISEASE, AND DEATH: being an Enquiry into the Progress of Medicine as a Practical Art. 8vo. cloth, 3s. 6d.

EDWARD ELLIS, M.D.
A PRACTICAL MANUAL OF THE DISEASES OF CHILDREN. With a Formulary. Crown 8vo. cloth, 6s.

SIR JAMES EYRE, M.D.

I.
THE STOMACH AND ITS DIFFICULTIES. Sixth Edition, by Mr. BEALE. Fcap. 8vo., 2s. 6d.

II.
PRACTICAL REMARKS ON SOME EXHAUSTING DISEASES. Second Edition. Post 8vo. cloth, 4s. 6d.

J. FAYRER, M.D., F.R.C.S., C.S.I.
CLINICAL SURGERY IN INDIA. With Engravings. 8vo. cloth, 16s.

SAMUEL FENWICK, M.D., M.R.C.P.

I.
THE MORBID STATES OF THE STOMACH AND DUODENUM, AND THEIR RELATIONS TO THE DISEASES OF OTHER ORGANS. With 10 Plates. 8vo. cloth, 12s.

II.
THE STUDENT'S GUIDE TO MEDICAL DIAGNOSIS. With 41 Engravings. Fcap. 8vo. cloth, 5s. 6d.

SIR WILLIAM FERGUSSON, BART., F.R.C.S., F.R.S.

I.
A SYSTEM OF PRACTICAL SURGERY; with numerous Illustrations on Wood. Fourth Edition. Fcap. 8vo. cloth, 12s. 6d.

II.
LECTURES ON THE PROGRESS OF ANATOMY AND SURGERY DURING THE PRESENT CENTURY. With numerous Engravings. 8vo. cloth, 10s. 6d.

SIR JOHN FIFE, F.R.C.S. AND DAVID URQUHART.

MANUAL OF THE TURKISH BATH. Heat a Mode of Cure and a Source of Strength for Men and Animals. With Engravings. Post 8vo. cloth, 5s.

W. H. FLOWER, F.R.C.S., F.R.S.

DIAGRAMS OF THE NERVES OF THE HUMAN BODY, exhibiting their Origin, Divisions, and Connexions, with their Distribution to the various Regions of the Cutaneous Surface, and to all the Muscles. Folio, containing Six Plates, 14s.

WILLIAM FLUX.

THE LAW TO REGULATE THE SALE OF POISONS WITHIN GREAT BRITAIN. Crown 8vo. cloth, 2s. 6d.

G. FOWNES, PH.D., F.R.S.

I.
A MANUAL OF CHEMISTRY; with 187 Illustrations on Wood. Tenth Edition. Fcap. 8vo. cloth, 14s.
Edited by H. Bence Jones, M.D., F.R.S., and Henry Watts, B.A., F.R.S.

II.
CHEMISTRY, AS EXEMPLIFYING THE WISDOM AND BENEFICENCE OF GOD. Second Edition. Fcap. 8vo. cloth, 4s. 6d.

III.
INTRODUCTION TO QUALITATIVE ANALYSIS. Post 8vo. cloth, 2s.

D. J. T. FRANCIS, M.D., F.R.C.P.

CHANGE OF CLIMATE; considered as a Remedy in Dyspeptic, Pulmonary, and other Chronic Affections; with an Account of the most Eligible Places of Residence for Invalids, at different Seasons of the Year. Post 8vo. cloth, 8s. 6d.

W. H. FULLER, M.D., F.R.C.P.

I.
ON DISEASES OF THE LUNGS AND AIR PASSAGES. Second Edition. 8vo. cloth, 12s. 6d.

II.
ON DISEASES OF THE HEART AND GREAT VESSELS. 8vo. cloth, 7s. 6d.

III.
ON RHEUMATISM, RHEUMATIC GOUT, AND SCIATICA: their Pathology, Symptoms, and Treatment. Third Edition. 8vo. cloth, 12s. 6d.

REMIGIUS FRESENIUS.
A SYSTEM OF INSTRUCTION IN CHEMICAL ANALYSIS,
Edited by ARTHUR VACHER.
    QUALITATIVE. Seventh Edition. 8vo. cloth, 9s.
    QUANTITATIVE. Fifth Edition. 8vo. cloth, 12s. 6d.

ROBERT GALLOWAY.
I.
THE FIRST STEP IN CHEMISTRY. With numerous Engravings. Fourth Edition. Fcap. 8vo. cloth, 6s. 6d.

II.
A KEY TO THE EXERCISES CONTAINED IN ABOVE. Fcap. 8vo., 2s. 6d.

III.
THE SECOND STEP IN CHEMISTRY; or, the Student's Guide to the Higher Branches of the Science. With Engravings. 8vo. cloth, 10s.

IV.
A MANUAL OF QUALITATIVE ANALYSIS. Fifth Edition. With Engravings. Post 8vo. cloth, 8s. 6d.

V.
CHEMICAL TABLES. On Five Large Sheets, for School and Lecture Rooms. Second Edition. 4s. 6d.

J. SAMPSON GAMGEE, M.R.C.S.
HISTORY OF A SUCCESSFUL CASE OF AMPUTATION AT THE HIP-JOINT (the limb 48-in. in circumference, 99 pounds weight). With 4 Photographs. 4to cloth, 10s. 6d.

F. J. GANT, F.R.C.S.
I.
THE PRINCIPLES OF SURGERY: Clinical, Medical, and Operative. With Engravings. 8vo. cloth, 18s.

II.
THE IRRITABLE BLADDER: its Causes and Curative Treatment. Second Edition, enlarged. Crown 8vo. cloth, 5s.

JOHN GAY, F.R.C.S.
ON VARICOSE DISEASE OF THE LOWER EXTREMITIES. LETTSOMIAN LECTURES. With Plates. 8vo. cloth, 5s.

SIR DUNCAN GIBB, BART., M.D.
I.
ON DISEASES OF THE THROAT AND WINDPIPE, as reflected by the Laryngoscope. Second Edition. With 116 Engravings. Post 8vo. cloth, 10s. 6d.

II.
THE LARYNGOSCOPE IN DISEASES OF THE THROAT, with a Chapter on RHINOSCOPY. Third Edition, with Engravings. Crown 8vo., cloth, 5s.

C. A. GORDON, M.D., C.B.
I.
ARMY HYGIENE. 8vo. cloth, 20s.

II.
CHINA, FROM A MEDICAL POINT OF VIEW; IN 1860 AND 1861; With a Chapter on Nagasaki as a Sanatarium. 8vo. cloth, 10s. 6d.

WILLIAM GAIRDNER, M.D.
ON GOUT; its History, its Causes, and its Cure. Fourth Edition. Post 8vo. cloth, 8s. 6d.

MICHAEL C. GRABHAM, M.D., M.R.C.P.
THE CLIMATE AND RESOURCES OF MADEIRA, as regarding chiefly the Necessities of Consumption and the Welfare of Invalids. With Map and Engravings. Crown 8vo. cloth, 5s.

R. J. GRAVES, M.D., F.R.S.
STUDIES IN PHYSIOLOGY AND MEDICINE. Edited by Dr. Stokes. With Portrait and Memoir. 8vo. cloth, 14s.

T. GRIFFITHS.
CHEMISTRY OF THE FOUR SEASONS — Spring, Summer, Autumn, Winter. Illustrated with Engravings on Wood. Second Edition. Foolscap 8vo. cloth, 7s. 6d.

JAMES M. GULLY, M.D.
THE SIMPLE TREATMENT OF DISEASE; deduced from the Methods of Expectancy and Revulsion. 18mo. cloth, 4s.

W. A. GUY, M.B., F.R.S., AND JOHN HARLEY, M.D., F.R.C.P.
HOOPER'S PHYSICIAN'S VADE-MECUM; OR, MANUAL OF THE PRINCIPLES AND PRACTICE OF PHYSIC. Seventh Edition. With Engravings. Foolscap 8vo. cloth, 12s. 6d.

GUY'S HOSPITAL REPORTS. Third Series. Vol. XV., 8vo. 7s. 6d.

S. O. HABERSHON, M.D., F.R.C.P.
I.
ON DISEASES OF THE ABDOMEN, comprising those of the Stomach and other Parts of the Alimentary Canal, Œsophagus, Stomach, Cæcum, Intestines, and Peritoneum. Second Edition, with Plates. 8vo. cloth, 14s.
II.
ON THE INJURIOUS EFFECTS OF MERCURY IN THE TREATMENT OF DISEASE. Post 8vo. cloth, 3s. 6d.

C. RADCLYFFE HALL, F.R.C.P.
TORQUAY IN ITS MEDICAL ASPECT AS A RESORT FOR PULMONARY INVALIDS. Post 8vo. cloth, 5s.

MARSHALL HALL, M.D., F.R.S.
I.
PRONE AND POSTURAL RESPIRATION IN DROWNING AND OTHER FORMS OF APNŒA OR SUSPENDED RESPIRATION. Post 8vo. cloth, 5s.
II.
PRACTICAL OBSERVATIONS AND SUGGESTIONS IN MEDICINE. Second Series. Post 8vo. cloth, 8s. 6d.

REV. T F. HARDWICH.
A MANUAL OF PHOTOGRAPHIC CHEMISTRY. With Engravings. Seventh Edition. Foolscap 8vo. cloth, 7s. 6d.

J. BOWER HARRISON, M.D., M.R.C.P.

I.
LETTERS TO A YOUNG PRACTITIONER ON THE DISEASES OF CHILDREN. Foolscap 8vo. cloth, 3s.

II.
ON THE CONTAMINATION OF WATER BY THE POISON OF LEAD, and its Effects on the Human Body. Foolscap 8vo. cloth, 3s. 6d.

GEORGE HARTWIG, M.D.

I.
ON SEA BATHING AND SEA AIR. Second Edition. Fcap. 8vo., 2s. 6d.

II.
ON THE PHYSICAL EDUCATION OF CHILDREN. Fcap. 8vo., 2s. 6d.

A. H. HASSALL, M.D.

THE URINE, IN HEALTH AND DISEASE; being an Explanation of the Composition of the Urine, and of the Pathology and Treatment of Urinary and Renal Disorders. Second Edition. With 79 Engravings (23 Coloured). Post 8vo. cloth, 12s. 6d.

ALFRED HAVILAND, M.R.C.S.

CLIMATE, WEATHER, AND DISEASE; being a Sketch of the Opinions of the most celebrated Ancient and Modern Writers with regard to the Influence of Climate and Weather in producing Disease. With Four coloured Engravings. 8vo. cloth, 7s.

W. HAYCOCK, M.R.C.V.S.

HORSES; HOW THEY OUGHT TO BE SHOD: being a plain and practical Treatise on the Principles and Practice of the Farrier's Art. With 14 Plates. Cloth, 7s. 6d.

F. W. HEADLAND, M.D., F.R.C.P.

I.
ON THE ACTION OF MEDICINES IN THE SYSTEM. Fourth Edition. 8vo. cloth, 14s.

II.
A MEDICAL HANDBOOK; comprehending such Information on Medical and Sanitary Subjects as is desirable in Educated Persons. Second Thousand. Foolscap 8vo. cloth, 5s.

J. N. HEALE, M.D., M.R.C.P.

I.
A TREATISE ON THE PHYSIOLOGICAL ANATOMY OF THE LUNGS. With Engravings. 8vo. cloth, 8s.

II.
A TREATISE ON VITAL CAUSES. 8vo. cloth, 9s.

CHRISTOPHER HEATH, F.R.C.S.

I.
PRACTICAL ANATOMY: a Manual of Dissections. With numerous Engravings. Second Edition. Fcap. 8vo. cloth, 12s. 6d.

II.
A MANUAL OF MINOR SURGERY AND BANDAGING, FOR THE USE OF HOUSE-SURGEONS, DRESSERS, AND JUNIOR PRACTITIONERS. With Illustrations. Third Edition. Fcap. 8vo. cloth, 5s.

III.
INJURIES AND DISEASES OF THE JAWS. JACKSONIAN PRIZE ESSAY. With Engravings. 8vo. cloth, 12s.

JOHN HIGGINBOTTOM, F.R.S., F.R.C.S.E.

A PRACTICAL ESSAY ON THE USE OF THE NITRATE OF SILVER IN THE TREATMENT OF INFLAMMATION, WOUNDS, AND ULCERS. Third Edition, 8vo. cloth, 6s.

WILLIAM HINDS, M.D.

THE HARMONIES OF PHYSICAL SCIENCE IN RELATION TO THE HIGHER SENTIMENTS; with Observations on Medical Studies, and on the Moral and Scientific Relations of Medical Life. Post 8vo. cloth, 4s.

J. A. HINGESTON, M.R.C.S.

TOPICS OF THE DAY, MEDICAL, SOCIAL, AND SCIENTIFIC. Crown 8vo. cloth, 7s. 6d.

RICHARD HODGES, M.D.

THE NATURE, PATHOLOGY, AND TREATMENT OF PUERPERAL CONVULSIONS. Crown 8vo. cloth, 3s.

DECIMUS HODGSON, M.D.

THE PROSTATE GLAND, AND ITS ENLARGEMENT IN OLD AGE. With 12 Plates. Royal 8vo. cloth, 6s.

JABEZ HOGG, M.R.C.S.

A MANUAL OF OPHTHALMOSCOPIC SURGERY; being a Practical Treatise on the Use of the Ophthalmoscope in Diseases of the Eye. Third Edition. With Coloured Plates. 8vo. cloth, 10s. 6d.

LUTHER HOLDEN, F.R.C.S.

I.
HUMAN OSTEOLOGY: with Plates, showing the Attachments of the Muscles. Fourth Edition. 8vo. cloth, 16s.

II.
A MANUAL OF THE DISSECTION OF THE HUMAN BODY. With Engravings on Wood. Third Edition. 8vo. cloth, 16s.

BARNARD HOLT, F.R.C.S.

ON THE IMMEDIATE TREATMENT OF STRICTURE OF THE URETHRA. Third Edition, Enlarged. 8vo. cloth, 6s.

SIR CHARLES HOOD, M.D.
SUGGESTIONS FOR THE FUTURE PROVISION OF CRIMINAL LUNATICS. 8vo. cloth, 5s. 6d.

P. HOOD M.D.
THE SUCCESSFUL TREATMENT OF SCARLET FEVER; also, OBSERVATIONS ON THE PATHOLOGY AND TREATMENT OF CROWING INSPIRATIONS OF INFANTS. Post 8vo. cloth, 5s.

JOHN HORSLEY.
A CATECHISM OF CHEMICAL PHILOSOPHY; being a Familiar Exposition of the Principles of Chemistry and Physics. With Engravings on Wood. Designed for the Use of Schools and Private Teachers. Post 8vo. cloth, 6s. 6d.

JAMES A. HORTON, M.D.
PHYSICAL AND MEDICAL CLIMATE AND METEOROLOGY OF THE WEST COAST OF AFRICA. 8vo. cloth, 10s.

LUKE HOWARD, F.R.S.
ESSAY ON THE MODIFICATIONS OF CLOUDS. Third Edition, by W. D. and E. Howard. With 6 Lithographic Plates, from Pictures by Kenyon. 4to. cloth, 10s. 6d.

A. HAMILTON HOWE, M.D.
A THEORETICAL INQUIRY INTO THE PHYSICAL CAUSE OF EPIDEMIC DISEASES. Accompanied with Tables. 8vo. cloth, 7s.

C. W. HUFELAND.
THE ART OF PROLONGING LIFE. Second Edition. Edited by Erasmus Wilson, F.R.S. Foolscap 8vo., 2s. 6d.

W. CURTIS HUGMAN, F.R.C.S.
ON HIP-JOINT DISEASE; with reference especially to Treatment by Mechanical Means for the Relief of Contraction and Deformity of the Affected Limb. With Plates. Re-issue, enlarged. 8vo. cloth, 3s. 6d.

J. W. HULKE, F.R.C.S., F.R.S.
A PRACTICAL TREATISE ON THE USE OF THE OPHTHALMOSCOPE. Being the Jacksonian Prize Essay for 1859. Royal 8vo. cloth, 8s.

HENRY HUNT, F.R.C.P.
ON HEARTBURN AND INDIGESTION. 8vo. cloth, 5s.

G. Y. HUNTER, M.R.C.S.
BODY AND MIND: the Nervous System and its Derangements. Fcap. 8vo. cloth, 3s. 6d.

JONATHAN HUTCHINSON, F.R.C.S.
A CLINICAL MEMOIR ON CERTAIN DISEASES OF THE EYE AND EAR, CONSEQUENT ON INHERITED SYPHILIS; with an appended Chapter of Commentaries on the Transmission of Syphilis from Parent to Offspring, and its more remote Consequences. With Plates and Woodcuts, 8vo. cloth, 9s.

T. H. HUXLEY, LL.D., F.R.S.
INTRODUCTION TO THE CLASSIFICATION OF ANIMALS. With Engravings. 8vo. cloth, 6s.

THOMAS INMAN, M.D., M.R.C.P.
I.
ON MYALGIA: ITS NATURE, CAUSES, AND TREATMENT; being a Treatise on Painful and other Affections of the Muscular System. Second Edition. 8vo. cloth, 9s.

II.
FOUNDATION FOR A NEW THEORY AND PRACTICE OF MEDICINE. Second Edition. Crown 8vo. cloth, 10s.

JAMES JAGO, M.D.OXON., A.B.CANTAB.
ENTOPTICS, WITH ITS USES IN PHYSIOLOGY AND MEDICINE. With 54 Engravings. Crown 8vo. cloth, 5s.

M. PROSSER JAMES, M.D., M.R.C.P.
SORE-THROAT: ITS NATURE, VARIETIES, AND TREATMENT; including the Use of the LARYNGOSCOPE as an Aid to Diagnosis. Second Edition, with numerous Engravings. Post 8vo. cloth, 5s.

F. E. JENCKEN, M.D., M.R.C.P.
THE CHOLERA: ITS ORIGIN, IDIOSYNCRACY, AND TREATMENT. Fcap. 8vo. cloth, 2s. 6d.

C. HANDFIELD JONES, M.B., F.R.C.P., F.R.S.
STUDIES ON FUNCTIONAL NERVOUS DISORDERS. Second Edition, much enlarged. 8vo. cloth, 18s.

H. BENCE JONES, M.D., F.R.C.P., F.R.S.
I.
LECTURES ON SOME OF THE APPLICATIONS OF CHEMISTRY AND MECHANICS TO PATHOLOGY AND THERAPEUTICS. 8vo. cloth, 12s.

II.
CROONIAN LECTURES ON MATTER AND FORCE. Fcap. 8vo. cloth, 5s.

C. HANDFIELD JONES, M.B., F.R.S., & E. H. SIEVEKING, M.D., F.R.C.P.
A MANUAL OF PATHOLOGICAL ANATOMY. Illustrated with numerous Engravings on Wood. Foolscap 8vo. cloth, 12s. 6d.

JAMES JONES, M.D., M.R.C.P.

ON THE USE OF PERCHLORIDE OF IRON AND OTHER CHALYBEATE SALTS IN THE TREATMENT OF CONSUMPTION. Crown 8vo. cloth, 3s. 6d.

T. WHARTON JONES, F.R.C.S., F.R.S.

I.

A MANUAL OF THE PRINCIPLES AND PRACTICE OF OPHTHALMIC MEDICINE AND SURGERY; with Nine Coloured Plates and 173 Wood Engravings. Third Edition, thoroughly revised. Foolscap 8vo. cloth, 12s. 6d.

II.

THE WISDOM AND BENEFICENCE OF THE ALMIGHTY, AS DISPLAYED IN THE SENSE OF VISION. Actonian Prize Essay. With Illustrations on Steel and Wood. Foolscap 8vo. cloth, 4s. 6d.

III.

DEFECTS OF SIGHT AND HEARING: their Nature, Causes, Prevention, and General Management. Second Edition, with Engravings. Fcap. 8vo. 2s. 6d.

IV.

A CATECHISM OF THE MEDICINE AND SURGERY OF THE EYE AND EAR. For the Clinical Use of Hospital Students. Fcap. 8vo. 2s. 6d.

V.

A CATECHISM OF THE PHYSIOLOGY AND PHILOSOPHY OF BODY, SENSE, AND MIND. For Use in Schools and Colleges. Fcap. 8vo., 2s. 6d.

U. J. KAY-SHUTTLEWORTH, M.P.

FIRST PRINCIPLES OF MODERN CHEMISTRY: a Manual of Inorganic Chemistry. Second Edition. Crown 8vo. cloth, 4s. 6d.

DR. LAENNEC.

A MANUAL OF AUSCULTATION AND PERCUSSION. Translated and Edited by J. B. Sharpe, M.R.C.S. 3s.

SIR WM. LAWRENCE, BART., F.R.S.

I.

LECTURES ON SURGERY. 8vo. cloth, 16s.

II.

A TREATISE ON RUPTURES. The Fifth Edition, considerably enlarged. 8vo. cloth, 16s.

ARTHUR LEARED, M.D., M.R.C.P.

IMPERFECT DIGESTION: ITS CAUSES AND TREATMENT. Fifth Edition. Foolscap 8vo. cloth, 4s. 6d.

HENRY LEE, F.R.C.S.

PRACTICAL PATHOLOGY. Third Edition, in 2 Vols. Containing Lectures on Suppurative Fever, Diseases of the Veins, Hæmorrhoidal Tumours, Diseases of the Rectum, Syphilis, Gonorrhœal Ophthalmia, &c. 8vo. cloth, 10s. each vol.

EDWIN LEE, M.D.

I.
THE EFFECT OF CLIMATE ON TUBERCULOUS DISEASE, with Notices of the chief Foreign Places of Winter Resort. Small 8vo. cloth, 4s. 6d.

II.
THE WATERING PLACES OF ENGLAND, CONSIDERED with Reference to their Medical Topography. Fourth Edition. Fcap. 8vo. cloth, 7s. 6d.

III.
THE BATHS OF FRANCE. Fourth Edition. Fcap. 8vo. cloth, 4s. 6d.

IV.
THE BATHS OF GERMANY. Fourth Edition. Post 8vo. cloth, 7s.

V.
THE BATHS OF SWITZERLAND. 12mo. cloth, 3s. 6d.

VI.
HOMŒOPATHY AND HYDROPATHY IMPARTIALLY APPRECIATED. Fourth Edition. Post 8vo. cloth, 3s.

ROBERT LEE, M.D, F.R.O.P., F.R.S.

I.
CONSULTATIONS IN MIDWIFERY. Foolscap 8vo. cloth, 4s. 6d.

II.
A TREATISE ON THE SPECULUM; with Three Hundred Cases. 8vo. cloth, 4s. 6d.

III.
CLINICAL REPORTS OF OVARIAN AND UTERINE DISEASES, with Commentaries. Foolscap 8vo. cloth, 6s. 6d.

IV.
CLINICAL MIDWIFERY: comprising the Histories of 545 Cases of Difficult, Preternatural, and Complicated Labour, with Commentaries. Second Edition. Foolscap 8vo. cloth, 5s.

WM. LEISHMAN, M.D., F.F.P.S.

THE MECHANISM OF PARTURITION: An Essay, Historical and Critical. With Engravings. 8vo. cloth, 5s.

F. HARWOOD LESCHER.

THE ELEMENTS OF PHARMACY. 8vo. cloth, 7s. 6d.

ROBERT LISTON, F.R.S.

PRACTICAL SURGERY. Fourth Edition. 8vo. cloth, 22s.

D. D. LOGAN, M.D., M.R.C.P.LOND.

ON OBSTINATE DISEASES OF THE SKIN. Fcap. 8vo. cloth, 2s. 6d.

LONDON HOSPITAL.

CLINICAL LECTURES AND REPORTS BY THE MEDICAL AND SURGICAL STAFF. With Illustrations. Vols. I. to IV. 8vo. cloth, 7s. 6d.

LONDON MEDICAL SOCIETY OF OBSERVATION.
WHAT TO OBSERVE AT THE BED-SIDE, AND AFTER DEATH. Published by Authority. Second Edition. Foolscap 8vo. cloth, 4s. 6d.

HENRY LOWNDES, M.R.C.S.
AN ESSAY ON THE MAINTENANCE OF HEALTH. Fcap. 8vo. cloth, 2s. 6d.

MORELL MACKENZIE, M.D. LOND., M.R.C.P.
HOARSENESS, LOSS OF VOICE, AND STRIDULOUS BREATHING in relation to NERVO-MUSCULAR AFFECTIONS of the LARYNX. Second Edition. Fully Illustrated. 8vo. 2s. 6d.

DANIEL MACLACHLAN, M.D., F.R.C.P.L.
THE DISEASES AND INFIRMITIES OF ADVANCED LIFE. 8vo. cloth, 16s.

A. C. MACLEOD, M.R.C.P.LOND.
ACHOLIC DISEASES; comprising Jaundice, Diarrhœa, Dysentery, and Cholera. Post 8vo. cloth, 5s. 6d.

GEORGE H. B. MACLEOD, M.D., F.R.C.S.EDIN.
I.
OUTLINES OF SURGICAL DIAGNOSIS. 8vo. cloth, 12s. 6d.

II.
NOTES ON THE SURGERY OF THE CRIMEAN WAR; with REMARKS on GUN-SHOT WOUNDS. 8vo. cloth, 10s. 6d.

WM. MACLEOD, M.D., F.R.C.P.EDIN.
THE THEORY OF THE TREATMENT OF DISEASE ADOPTED AT BEN RHYDDING. Fcap. 8vo. cloth, 2s. 6d.

JOSEPH MACLISE, F.R.C.S.
I.
SURGICAL ANATOMY. A Series of Dissections, illustrating the Principal Regions of the Human Body. Second Edition, folio, cloth, £3. 12s.; half-morocco, £4. 4s.

II.
ON DISLOCATIONS AND FRACTURES. This Work is Uniform with "Surgical Anatomy;" folio, cloth, £2. 10s.; half-morocco, £2. 17s.

N. C. MACNAMARA.
I.
A MANUAL OF THE DISEASES OF THE EYE. With Coloured Plates. Fcap. 8vo. cloth, 12s. 6d.

II.
A TREATISE ON ASIATIC CHOLERA; with Maps. 8vo. cloth, 16s.

WM. MARCET, M.D., F.R.C.P., F.R.S.
ON CHRONIC ALCOHOLIC INTOXICATION; with an INQUIRY INTO THE INFLUENCE OF THE ABUSE OF ALCOHOL AS A PREDISPOSING CAUSE OF DISEASE. Second Edition, much enlarged. Foolscap 8vo. cloth, 4s. 6d.

MESSRS. CHURCHILL & SONS' PUBLICATIONS.

J. MACPHERSON, M.D.

CHOLERA IN ITS HOME; with a Sketch of the Pathology and Treatment of the Disease. Crown 8vo. cloth, 5s.

W. O. MARKHAM, M.D., F.R.C.P.

I.
DISEASES OF THE HEART: THEIR PATHOLOGY, DIAGNOSIS, AND TREATMENT. Second Edition. Post 8vo. cloth, 6s.

II.
SKODA ON AUSCULTATION AND PERCUSSION. Post 8vo. cloth, 6s.

III.
BLEEDING AND CHANGE IN TYPE OF DISEASES. Gulstonian Lectures for 1864. Crown 8vo. 2s. 6d.

ALEXANDER MARSDEN, M.D., F.R.C.S.

A NEW AND SUCCESSFUL MODE OF TREATING CERTAIN FORMS OF CANCER; to which is prefixed a Practical and Systematic Description of all the Varieties of this Disease. With Coloured Plates. 8vo. cloth, 6s. 6d.

SIR RANALD MARTIN, C.B., F.R.C.S., F.R.S.

INFLUENCE OF TROPICAL CLIMATES IN PRODUCING THE ACUTE ENDEMIC DISEASES OF EUROPEANS; including Practical Observations on their Chronic Sequelæ under the Influences of the Climate of Europe. Second Edition, much enlarged. 8vo. cloth, 20s.

P. MARTYN, M.D.LOND.

HOOPING-COUGH; ITS PATHOLOGY AND TREATMENT. With Engravings. 8vo. cloth, 2s. 6d.

C. F. MAUNDER, F.R.C.S.

OPERATIVE SURGERY. With 158 Engravings. Post 8vo. 6s.

R. G. MAYNE, M.D., LL.D.

I.
AN EXPOSITORY LEXICON OF THE TERMS, ANCIENT AND MODERN, IN MEDICAL AND GENERAL SCIENCE. 8vo. cloth, £2. 10s.

II.
A MEDICAL VOCABULARY; or, an Explanation of all Names, Synonymes, Terms, and Phrases used in Medicine and the relative branches of Medical Science. Third Edition. Fcap. 8vo. cloth, 8s. 6d.

EDWARD MERYON, M.D., F.R.C.P.

PATHOLOGICAL AND PRACTICAL RESEARCHES ON THE VARIOUS FORMS OF PARALYSIS. 8vo. cloth, 6s.

W. J. MOORE, M.D.

I.
HEALTH IN THE TROPICS; or, Sanitary Art applied to Europeans in India. 8vo. cloth, 9s.

II.
A MANUAL OF THE DISEASES OF INDIA. Fcap. 8vo. cloth, 5s.

JAMES MORRIS, M.D.LOND.

I.
GERMINAL MATTER AND THE CONTACT THEORY: An Essay on the Morbid Poisons. Second Edition. Crown 8vo. cloth, 4s. 6d.

II.
IRRITABILITY: Popular and Practical Sketches of Common Morbid States and Conditions bordering on Disease; with Hints for Management, Alleviation, and Cure. Crown 8vo. cloth, 4s. 6d.

G. J. MULDER.

THE CHEMISTRY OF WINE. Edited by H. BENCE JONES, M.D., F.R.S. Fcap. 8vo. cloth, 6s.

W. MURRAY, M.D. M.R.C.P.

EMOTIONAL DISORDERS OF THE SYMPATHETIC SYSTEM OF NERVES. Crown 8vo. cloth, 3s. 6d.

W. B. MUSHET, M.B., M.R.C.P.

ON APOPLEXY, AND ALLIED AFFECTIONS OF THE BRAIN. 8vo. cloth, 7s.

GEORGE NAYLER, F.R.C.S.

ON THE DISEASES OF THE SKIN. With Plates. 8vo. cloth, 10s. 6d.

J. BIRKBECK NEVINS, M.D.

THE PRESCRIBER'S ANALYSIS OF THE BRITISH PHARMACOPEIA of 1867. 32mo. cloth, 3s. 6d.

H. M. NOAD, PH.D., F.R.S.

THE INDUCTION COIL, being a Popular Explanation of the Electrical Principles on which it is constructed. Third Edition. With Engravings. Fcap. 8vo. cloth, 3s.

DANIEL NOBLE, M.D., F.R.C.P.

THE HUMAN MIND IN ITS RELATIONS WITH THE BRAIN AND NERVOUS SYSTEM. Post 8vo. cloth, 4s. 6d.

SELBY NORTON, M.D.

INFANTILE DISEASES: their Causes, Prevention, and Treatment, showing by what Means the present Mortality may be greatly reduced. Fcap. 8vo. cloth, 2s. 6d.

THOMAS NUNNELEY, F.R.C.S.

I.
ON THE ORGANS OF VISION: THEIR ANATOMY AND PHYSIOLOGY. With Plates, 8vo. cloth, 15s.

II.
A TREATISE ON THE NATURE, CAUSES, AND TREATMENT OF ERYSIPELAS. 8vo. cloth, 10s. 6d.

FRANCIS OPPERT, M.D., M.R.C.P.

I.
HOSPITALS, INFIRMARIES, AND DISPENSARIES; their Construction, Interior Arrangement, and Management, with Descriptions of existing Institutions. With 58 Engravings. Royal 8vo. cloth, 10s. 6d.

II.
VISCERAL AND HEREDITARY SYPHILIS. 8vo. cloth, 5s.

LANGSTON PARKER, F.R.C.S.

THE MODERN TREATMENT OF SYPHILITIC DISEASES, both Primary and Secondary; comprising the Treatment of Constitutional and Confirmed Syphilis, by a safe and successful Method. Fourth Edition, 8vo. cloth, 10s.

E. A. PARKES, M.D., F.R.C.P., F.R.S.

I.
A MANUAL OF PRACTICAL HYGIENE; intended especially for the Medical Officers of the Army. With Plates and Woodcuts. 3rd Edition, 8vo. cloth, 16s.

II.
THE URINE: ITS COMPOSITION IN HEALTH AND DISEASE, AND UNDER THE ACTION OF REMEDIES. 8vo. cloth, 12s.

JOHN PARKIN, M.D., F.R.C.S.

I.
THE ANTIDOTAL TREATMENT AND PREVENTION OF THE EPIDEMIC CHOLERA. Third Edition. 8vo. cloth, 7s. 6d.

II.
THE CAUSATION AND PREVENTION OF DISEASE; with the Laws regulating the Extrication of Malaria from the Surface, and its Diffusion in the surrounding Air. 8vo. cloth, 5s.

JAMES PART, F.R.C.S.
THE MEDICAL AND SURGICAL POCKET CASE BOOK, for the Registration of important Cases in Private Practice, and to assist the Student of Hospital Practice. Second Edition. 2s. 6d.

JOHN PATTERSON, M.D.
EGYPT AND THE NILE AS A WINTER RESORT FOR PULMONARY AND OTHER INVALIDS. Fcap. 8vo. cloth, 3s.

F. W. PAVY, M.D., F.R.S., F.R.C.P.

I.
DIABETES: RESEARCHES ON ITS NATURE AND TREATMENT. Second Edition. With Engravings. 8vo. cloth, 10s.

II.
DIGESTION: ITS DISORDERS AND THEIR TREATMENT. Second Edition. 8vo. cloth, 8s. 6d.

T. B. PEACOCK, M.D., F.R.C.P.

I.
ON MALFORMATIONS OF THE HUMAN HEART. With Original Cases and Illustrations. Second Edition. With 8 Plates. 8vo. cloth, 10s.

II.
ON SOME OF THE CAUSES AND EFFECTS OF VALVULAR DISEASE OF THE HEART. With Engravings. 8vo. cloth, 5s.

W. H. PEARSE, M.D.EDIN.
NOTES ON HEALTH IN CALCUTTA AND BRITISH EMIGRANT SHIPS, including Ventilation, Diet, and Disease. Fcap. 8vo. 2s.

JONATHAN PEREIRA, M.D., F.R.S.
SELECTA E PRÆSCRIPTIS. Fifteenth Edition. 24mo. cloth, 5s.

JAMES H. PICKFORD, M.D.
HYGIENE; or, Health as Depending upon the Conditions of the Atmosphere, Food and Drinks, Motion and Rest, Sleep and Wakefulness, Secretions, Excretions, and Retentions, Mental Emotions, Clothing, Bathing, &c. Vol. I. 8vo. cloth, 9s.

MESSRS. CHURCHILL & SONS' PUBLICATIONS.

WILLIAM PIRRIE, M.D., C.M;, F.R.S.E.
THE PRINCIPLES AND PRACTICE OF SURGERY. With numerous Engravings on Wood. Second Edition. 8vo. cloth, 24s.

WILLIAM PIRRIE, M.D.
ON HAY ASTHMA, AND THE AFFECTION TERMED HAY FEVER. Fcap. 8vo. cloth, 2s. 6d.

HENRY POWER, F.R.C.S., M.B.LOND.
ILLUSTRATIONS OF SOME OF THE PRINCIPAL DISEASES OF THE EYE: With an Account of their Symptoms, Pathology and Treatment. Twelve Coloured Plates. 8vo. cloth, 20s.

HENRY F. A. PRATT, M.D., M.R.C.P.

I.
THE GENEALOGY OF CREATION, newly Translated from the Unpointed Hebrew Text of the Book of Genesis, showing the General Scientific Accuracy of the Cosmogony of Moses and the Philosophy of Creation. 8vo. cloth, 14s.

II.
ON ECCENTRIC AND CENTRIC FORCE: A New Theory of Projection. With Engravings. 8vo. cloth, 10s.

III.
ON ORBITAL MOTION: The Outlines of a System of Physical Astronomy. With Diagrams. 8vo. cloth, 7s. 6d.

IV.
ASTRONOMICAL INVESTIGATIONS. The Cosmical Relations of the Revolution of the Lunar Apsides. Oceanic Tides. With Engravings. 8vo. cloth, 5s.

V.
THE ORACLES OF GOD: An Attempt at a Re-interpretation. Part I. The Revealed Cosmos. 8vo. cloth, 10s.

THE PRESCRIBER'S PHARMACOPŒIA; containing all the Medicines in the British Pharmacopœia, arranged in Classes according to their Action, with their Composition and Doses. By a Practising Physician. Fifth Edition. 32mo. cloth, 2s. 6d.; roan tuck (for the pocket), 3s. 6d.

JOHN ROWLISON PRETTY, M.D.
AIDS DURING LABOUR, including the Administration of Chloroform, the Management of Placenta and Post-partum Hæmorrhage. Fcap. 8vo. cloth, 4s. 6d.

P. C. PRICE, F.R.C.S.
AN ESSAY ON EXCISION OF THE KNEE-JOINT. With Coloured Plates. With Memoir of the Author and Notes by Henry Smith, F.R.C.S. Royal 8vo. cloth, 14s.

MESSRS. CHURCHILL & SONS' PUBLICATIONS.

LAKE PRICE.
PHOTOGRAPHIC MANIPULATION; A Manual treating of the Practice of the Art, and its various Applications to Nature. With numerous Engravings. Second Edition. Crown 8vo. cloth, 6s. 6d.

W. O. PRIESTLEY, M.D., F.R.C.P.
LECTURES ON THE DEVELOPMENT OF THE GRAVID UTERUS. 8vo. cloth, 5s. 6d.

GEORGE RAINEY, M.R.C.S.
ON THE MODE OF FORMATION OF SHELLS OF ANIMALS, OF BONE, AND OF SEVERAL OTHER STRUCTURES, by a Process of Molecular Coalescence, Demonstrable in certain Artificially-formed Products. Fcap. 8vo. cloth, 4s. 6d.

ROBERT RAMSAY AND J. OAKLEY COLES.
DEFORMITIES OF THE MOUTH, CONGENITAL AND ACCIDENTAL: Their Mechanical Treatment. With Illustrations. 8vo. cloth, 5s.

F. H. RAMSBOTHAM, M.D., F.R.C.P.
THE PRINCIPLES AND PRACTICE OF OBSTETRIC MEDICINE AND SURGERY. Illustrated with One Hundred and Twenty Plates on Steel and Wood; forming one thick handsome volume. Fifth Edition. 8vo. cloth, 22s.

THOMAS READE, M.B.T.C.D., L.R.C.S.I.
SYPHILITIC AFFECTIONS OF THE NERVOUS SYSTEM, AND A CASE OF SYMMETRICAL MUSCULAR ATROPHY; with other Contributions to the Pathology of the Spinal Marrow. Post 8vo. cloth, 5s.

THEOPHILUS REDWOOD, PH.D.
A SUPPLEMENT TO THE PHARMACOPŒIA: A concise but comprehensive Dispensatory, and Manual of Facts and Formulæ, for the use of Practitioners in Medicine and Pharmacy. Third Edition. 8vo. cloth, 22s.

DU BOIS REYMOND.
ANIMAL ELECTRICITY; Edited by H. BENCE JONES, M.D., F.R.S. With Fifty Engravings on Wood. Foolscap 8vo. cloth, 6s.

J. RUSSELL REYNOLDS, M.D.LOND., F.R.C.P., F.R.S.
I.
EPILEPSY: ITS SYMPTOMS, TREATMENT, AND RELATION TO OTHER CHRONIC CONVULSIVE DISEASES. 8vo. cloth, 10s.
II.
THE DIAGNOSIS OF DISEASES OF THE BRAIN, SPINAL CORD, AND THEIR APPENDAGES. 8vo. cloth, 8s.

B. W. RICHARDSON, M.D., F.R.C.P., F.R.S.
ON THE CAUSE OF THE COAGULATION OF THE BLOOD. Being the ASTLEY COOPER PRIZE ESSAY for 1856. With a Practical Appendix. 8vo. cloth, 16s.

WILLIAM ROBERTS, M.D., F.R.C.P.
AN ESSAY ON WASTING PALSY; being a Systematic Treatise on the Disease hitherto described as ATROPHIE MUSCULAIRE PROGRESSIVE. With Four Plates. 8vo. cloth, 5s.

O. H. F. ROUTH, D.M., M.R.C.P.
INFANT FEEDING, AND ITS INFLUENCE ON LIFE; Or, the Causes and Prevention of Infant Mortality. Second Edition. Fcap. 8vo. cloth, 6s.

W. H. ROBERTSON, M.D., M.R.C.P.
I.
THE NATURE AND TREATMENT OF GOUT. 8vo. cloth, 10s. 6d.

II.
A TREATISE ON DIET AND REGIMEN. Fourth Edition. 2 vols. 12s. post 8vo. cloth.

JAMES ROGERS, M.D.
ON THE PRESENT STATE OF THERAPEUTICS. With some Suggestions for placing it on a more scientific basis. 8vo. cloth, 6s. 6d.

JAMES ROGERS, M.D.
ON THE PRESENT STATE OF THERAPEUTICS. With some Suggestions for placing it on a more scientific basis. 8vo. cloth, 6s. 6d.

G. R. ROWE, M.D.
NERVOUS DISEASES, LIVER AND STOMACH COMPLAINTS, LOW SPIRITS, INDIGESTION, GOUT, ASTHMA, AND DISORDERS PRODUCED BY TROPICAL CLIMATES. With Cases. Sixteenth Edition. Fcap. 8vo. 2s. 6d.

J. F. ROYLE, M.D., F.R.S., AND F. W. HEADLAND, M.D., F.R.C.P.
A MANUAL OF MATERIA MEDICA AND THERAPEUTICS. With numerous Engravings on Wood. Fifth Edition. Fcap. 8vo. cloth, 12s. 6d.

W. B. RYAN, M.D.
INFANTICIDE: ITS LAW, PREVALENCE, PREVENTION, AND HISTORY. 8vo. cloth, 5s.

ST. GEORGE'S HOSPITAL REPORTS. Vols. I. to IV. 8vo. 7s. 6d.

T. P. SALT, BIRMINGHAM.
ON DEFORMITIES AND DEBILITIES OF THE LOWER EXTREMITIES AND THE MECHANICAL TREATMENT EMPLOYED IN THE PROMOTION OF THEIR CURE. With Plates. 8vo. cloth, 15s.

H. HYDE SALTER, M.D., F.R.C.P., F.R.S.
ASTHMA. Second Edition. 8vo. cloth, 10s.

W. H. O. SANKEY, M.D.LOND.
LECTURES ON MENTAL DISEASES. 8vo. cloth, 8s.

A. E. SANSOM, M.D.LOND., M.R.C.P.

I.
CHLOROFORM; ITS ACTION AND ADMINISTRATION. A Handbook. With Engravings. Crown 8vo. cloth, 5s.

II.
THE ARREST AND PREVENTION OF CHOLERA; being a Guide to the Antiseptic Treatment. Fcap. 8vo. cloth, 2s. 6d.

JOHN SAVORY, M.S.A.
A COMPENDIUM OF DOMESTIC MEDICINE, AND COMPANION TO THE MEDICINE CHEST; intended as a Source of Easy Reference for Clergymen, and for Families residing at a Distance from Professional Assistance. Seventh Edition. 12mo. cloth, 5s.

HERMANN SCHACHT.
THE MICROSCOPE, AND ITS APPLICATION TO VEGETABLE ANATOMY AND PHYSIOLOGY. Edited by FREDERICK CURREY, M.A. Post 8vo. cloth, 6s.

R. E. SCORESBY-JACKSON, M.D., F.R.S.E.
MEDICAL CLIMATOLOGY; or, a Topographical and Meteorological Description of the Localities resorted to in Winter and Summer by Invalids of various classes both at Home and Abroad. With an Isothermal Chart. Post 8vo. cloth, 12s.

R. H. SEMPLE M.D., M.R.C.P.
ON COUGH: its Causes, Varieties, and Treatment. With some practical Remarks on the Use of the Stethoscope as an aid to Diagnosis. Post 8vo. cloth, 4s. 6d.

E. J. SEYMOUR, M.D.

I.
ILLUSTRATIONS OF SOME OF THE PRINCIPAL DISEASES OF THE OVARIA: their Symptoms and Treatment; to which are prefixed Observations on the Structure and Functions of those parts in the Human Being and in Animals. On India paper. Folio, 16s.

II.
THE NATURE AND TREATMENT OF DROPSY; considered especially in reference to the Diseases of the Internal Organs of the Body, which most commonly produce it. 8vo. 5s.

THOS. SHAPTER, M.D., F.R.C.P.
THE CLIMATE OF THE SOUTH OF DEVON, AND ITS INFLUENCE UPON HEALTH. Second Edition, with Maps. 8vo. cloth, 10s. 6d.

E. SHAW, M.R.C.S.
THE MEDICAL REMEMBRANCER; OR, BOOK OF EMERGENCIES. Fifth Edition. Edited, with Additions, by JONATHAN HUTCHINSON, F.R.C.S. 32mo. cloth, 2s. 6d.

JOHN SHEA, M.D., B.A.
A MANUAL OF ANIMAL PHYSIOLOGY With an Appendix of Questions for the B.A. London and other Examinations. With Engravings. Foolscap 8vo. cloth, 5s. 6d.

CHARLES SHRIMPTON, M.D.
CHOLERA: ITS SEAT, NATURE, AND TREATMENT. With Engravings. 8vo. cloth, 4s. 6d.

FRANCIS SIBSON, M.D., F.R.C.P., F.R.S.
MEDICAL ANATOMY. With coloured Plates. Imperial folio. Complete in Seven Fasciculi. 5s. each.

E. H. SIEVEKING, M.D., F.R.C.P.
ON EPILEPSY AND EPILEPTIFORM SEIZURES: their Causes, Pathology, and Treatment. Second Edition. Post 8vo. cloth, 10s. 6d.

FREDERICK SIMMS, M.B., M.R.C.P.
A WINTER IN PARIS : being a few Experiences and Observations of French Medical and Sanitary Matters. Fcap. 8vo. cloth, 4s.

E. B. SINCLAIR, M.D., F.K.Q.C.P., AND G. JOHNSTON, M.D., F.K.Q.C.P.
PRACTICAL MIDWIFERY: Comprising an Account of 13,748 Deliveries, which occurred in the Dublin Lying-in Hospital, during a period of Seven Years. 8vo. cloth, 10s.

J. L. SIORDET, M.B.LOND., M.R.C.P.
MENTONE IN ITS MEDICAL ASPECT. Foolscap 8vo. cloth, 2s. 6d.

ALFRED SMEE, M.R.C.S., F.R.S.
GENERAL DEBILITY AND DEFECTIVE NUTRITION; their Causes, Consequences, and Treatment. Second Edition. Fcap. 8vo. cloth, 3s. 6d.

WM. SMELLIE, M.D.
OBSTETRIC PLATES; being a Selection from the more Important and Practical Illustrations contained in the Original Work. With Anatomical and Practical Directions. 8vo. cloth, 5s.

HENRY SMITH, F.R.C.S.
I.
ON STRICTURE OF THE URETHRA. 8vo. cloth, 7s. 6d.
II.
HÆMORRHOIDS AND PROLAPSUS OF THE RECTUM: Their Pathology and Treatment, with especial reference to the use of Nitric Acid. Third Edition. Fcap. 8vo. cloth, 3s.
III.
THE SURGERY OF THE RECTUM. Lettsomian Lectures. Second Edition. Fcap. 8vo. 3s. 6d.

JOHN SMITH, M.D., F.R.C.S.EDIN.
HANDBOOK OF DENTAL ANATOMY AND SURGERY, FOR THE USE OF STUDENTS AND PRACTITIONERS. Fcap. 8vo. cloth, 3s. 6d.

J. BARKER SMITH.
PHARMACEUTICAL GUIDE TO THE FIRST AND SECOND EXAMINATIONS. Crown 8vo. cloth, 6s. 6d.

W. TYLER SMITH, M.D., F.R.C.P.
A MANUAL OF OBSTETRICS, THEORETICAL AND PRACTICAL. Illustrated with 186 Engravings. Fcap. 8vo. cloth, 12s. 6d.

JOHN SNOW, M.D.
ON CHLOROFORM AND OTHER ANÆSTHETICS: THEIR ACTION AND ADMINISTRATION. Edited, with a Memoir of the Author, by Benjamin W. Richardson, M.D. 8vo. cloth, 10s. 6d.

J. VOSE SOLOMON, F.R.C.S.
TENSION OF THE EYEBALL; GLAUCOMA: some Account of the Operations practised in the 19th Century. 8vo. cloth, 4s.

STANHOPE TEMPLEMAN SPEER, M.D.
PATHOLOGICAL CHEMISTRY, IN ITS APPLICATION TO THE PRACTICE OF MEDICINE. Translated from the French of MM. Becquerel and Rodier. 8vo. cloth, reduced to 8s.

J. K. SPENDER, M.D. LOND.
A MANUAL OF THE PATHOLOGY AND TREATMENT OF ULCERS AND CUTANEOUS DISEASES OF THE LOWER LIMBS. 8vo. cloth, 4s.

PETER SQUIRE.
I.
A COMPANION TO THE BRITISH PHARMACOPŒIA. Seventh Edition. 8vo. cloth, 10s. 6d.
II.
THE PHARMACOPŒIAS OF THE LONDON HOSPITALS, arranged in Groups for easy Reference and Comparison. Second Edition. 18mo. cloth, 5s.

JOHN STEGGALL, M.D.
I.
A MEDICAL MANUAL FOR APOTHECARIES' HALL AND OTHER MEDICAL BOARDS. Twelfth Edition. 12mo. cloth, 10s.
II.
A MANUAL FOR THE COLLEGE OF SURGEONS; intended for the Use of Candidates for Examination and Practitioners. Second Edition. 12mo. cloth, 10s.
III.
FIRST LINES FOR CHEMISTS AND DRUGGISTS PREPARING FOR EXAMINATION AT THE PHARMACEUTICAL SOCIETY. Third Edition. 18mo. cloth, 3s. 6d.

WM. STOWE, M.R.C.S.
A TOXICOLOGICAL CHART, exhibiting at one view the Symptoms, Treatment, and Mode of Detecting the various Poisons, Mineral, Vegetable, and Animal. To which are added, concise Directions for the Treatment of Suspended Animation. Twelfth Edition. revised. On Sheet, 2s.; mounted on Roller, 5s.

FRANCIS SUTTON, F.C.S.
A SYSTEMATIC HANDBOOK OF VOLUMETRIC ANALYSIS; or, the Quantitative Estimation of Chemical Substances by Measure. With Engravings. Post 8vo. cloth, 7s. 6d.

W. P. SWAIN, F.R.C.S.
INJURIES AND DISEASES OF THE KNEE-JOINT, and their Treatment by Amputation and Excision Contrasted. Jacksonian Prize Essay. With 36 Engravings. 8vo. cloth, 9s.

J. G. SWAYNE, M.D.
OBSTETRIC APHORISMS FOR THE USE OF STUDENTS COMMENCING MIDWIFERY PRACTICE. With Engravings on Wood. Fourth Edition. Fcap. 8vo. cloth, 3s. 6d.

MESSRS. CHURCHILL & SONS' PUBLICATIONS. 35

SIR ALEXANDER TAYLOR, M.D., F.R.S.E.

THE CLIMATE OF PAU; with a Description of the Watering Places of the Pyrenees, and of the Virtues of their respective Mineral Sources in Disease. Third Edition. Post 8vo. cloth, 7s.

ALFRED S. TAYLOR, M.D., F.R.C.P., F.R.S.

I.
THE PRINCIPLES AND PRACTICE OF MEDICAL JURISPRUDENCE. With 176 Wood Engravings. 8vo. cloth, 28s.

II.
A MANUAL OF MEDICAL JURISPRUDENCE. Eighth Edition. With Engravings. Fcap. 8vo. cloth, 12s. 6d.

III.
ON POISONS, in relation to MEDICAL JURISPRUDENCE AND MEDICINE. Second Edition. Fcap. 8vo. cloth, 12s. 6d.

THEOPHILUS THOMPSON, M.D., F.R.C.P., F.R.S.

CLINICAL LECTURES ON PULMONARY CONSUMPTION; with additional Chapters by E. Symes Thompson, M.D. With Plates. 8vo. cloth, 7s. 6d.

ROBERT THOMAS, M.D.

THE MODERN PRACTICE OF PHYSIC; exhibiting the Symptoms, Causes, Morbid Appearances, and Treatment of the Diseases of all Climates. Eleventh Edition. Revised by ALGERNON FRAMPTON, M.D. 2 vols. 8vo. cloth, 28s.

SIR HENRY THOMPSON, F.R.C.S.

I.
STRICTURE OF THE URETHRA AND URINARY FISTULÆ; their Pathology and Treatment. Jacksonian Prize Essay. With Plates. Third Edition. 8vo. cloth, 10s.

II.
THE DISEASES OF THE PROSTATE; their Pathology and Treatment. With Plates. Third Edition. 8vo. cloth, 10s.

III.
PRACTICAL LITHOTOMY AND LITHOTRITY; or, An Inquiry into the best Modes of removing Stone from the Bladder. With numerous Engravings, 8vo. cloth, 9s.

IV.
CLINICAL LECTURES ON DISEASES OF THE URINARY ORGANS. With Engravings. Second Edition. Crown 8vo. cloth, 5s.

J. C. THOROWGOOD, M.D.LOND.

NOTES ON ASTHMA; its Nature, Forms and Treatment. Crown 8vo. cloth, 4s.

J. L. W. THUDICHUM, M.D., M.R.C.P.

I.
A TREATISE ON THE PATHOLOGY OF THE URINE, Including a complete Guide to its Analysis. With Plates, 8vo. cloth, 14s.

II.
A TREATISE ON GALL STONES: their Chemistry, Pathology, and Treatment. With Coloured Plates. 8vo. cloth, 10s.

E. J. TILT, M.D., M.R.C.P.

I.
ON UTERINE AND OVARIAN INFLAMMATION, AND ON THE PHYSIOLOGY AND DISEASES OF MENSTRUATION. Third Edition. 8vo. cloth, 12s.

II.
A HANDBOOK OF UTERINE THERAPEUTICS AND OF DISEASES OF WOMEN. Third Edition. Post 8vo. cloth, 10s.

III.
THE CHANGE OF LIFE IN HEALTH AND DISEASE: a Practical Treatise on the Nervous and other Affections incidental to Women at the Decline of Life. Second Edition. 8vo. cloth, 6s.

GODWIN W. TIMMS, M.D., M.R.C.P.

CONSUMPTION: its True Nature and Successful Treatment. Re-issue, enlarged. Crown 8vo. cloth, 10s.

ROBERT B. TODD, M.D., F.R.S.

I.
CLINICAL LECTURES ON THE PRACTICE OF MEDICINE. New Edition, in one Volume, Edited by Dr. Beale, 8vo. cloth, 18s.

II.
ON CERTAIN DISEASES OF THE URINARY ORGANS, AND ON DROPSIES. Fcap. 8vo. cloth, 6s.

JOHN TOMES, F.R.S.

A MANUAL OF DENTAL SURGERY. With 208 Engravings on Wood. Fcap. 8vo. cloth, 12s. 6d.

JAS. M. TURNBULL, M.D., M R.C.P.

I.
AN INQUIRY INTO THE CURABILITY OF CONSUMPTION, ITS PREVENTION, AND THE PROGRESS OF IMPROVEMENT IN THE TREATMENT. Third Edition. 8vo. cloth, 6s.

II.
A PRACTICAL TREATISE ON DISORDERS OF THE STOMACH with FERMENTATION; and on the Causes and Treatment of Indigestion, &c. 8vo. cloth, 6s.

R. V. TUSON, F.C.S.

A PHARMACOPŒIA; including the Outlines of Materia Medica and Therapeutics, for the Use of Practitioners and Students of Veterinary Medicine. Post 8vo. cloth, 7s.

ALEXR. TWEEDIE, M.D., F.R.C.P., F.R.S.

CONTINUED FEVERS: THEIR DISTINCTIVE CHARACTERS, PATHOLOGY, AND TREATMENT. With Coloured Plates. 8vo. cloth, 12s.

DR. UNDERWOOD.

TREATISE ON THE DISEASES OF CHILDREN. Tenth Edition, with Additions and Corrections by Henry Davies, M.D. 8vo. cloth, 15s.

VESTIGES OF THE NATURAL HISTORY OF CREATION. Eleventh Edition. Illustrated with 106 Engravings on Wood. 8vo. cloth, 7s. 6d.

J. L. C. SCHROEDER VAN DER KOLK.
THE PATHOLOGY AND THERAPEUTICS OF MENTAL
DISEASES. Translated by Mr. RUDALL, F.R.C.S. 8vo. cloth, 7s. 6d.

MISS VEITCH.
HANDBOOK FOR NURSES FOR THE SICK. Crown 8vo. cloth, 2s. 6d.

ROBERT WADE, F.R.C.S.
STRICTURE OF THE URETHRA, ITS COMPLICATIONS
AND EFFECTS; a Practical Treatise on the Nature and Treatment of those Affections. Fourth Edition. 8vo. cloth, 7s. 6d.

ADOLPHE WAHLTUCH, M.D.
A DICTIONARY OF MATERIA MEDICA AND THERA-
PEUTICS. 8vo. cloth, 15s.

J. WEST WALKER, M.B.LOND.
ON DIPHTHERIA AND DIPHTHERITIC DISEASES. Fcap. 8vo. cloth, 3s.

CHAS. WALLER, M.D.
ELEMENTS OF PRACTICAL MIDWIFERY; or, Companion to the Lying-in Room. Fourth Edition, with Plates. Fcap. cloth, 4s. 6d.

HAYNES WALTON, F.R.C.S.
SURGICAL DISEASES OF THE EYE. With Engravings on Wood. Second Edition. 8vo. cloth, 14s.

E. J. WARING, M.D., M.R.C.P.LOND.
I.
A MANUAL OF PRACTICAL THERAPEUTICS. Second Edition, Revised and Enlarged. Fcap. 8vo. cloth, 12s. 6d.

II.
THE TROPICAL RESIDENT AT HOME. Letters addressed to Europeans returning from India and the Colonies on Subjects connected with their Health and General Welfare. Crown 8vo. cloth, 5s.

A. T. H. WATERS, M.D., F.R.C.P.
I.
DISEASES OF THE CHEST. CONTRIBUTIONS TO THEIR CLINICAL HISTORY, PATHOLOGY, AND TREATMENT. With Plates. 8vo. cloth, 12s. 6d.
II.
THE ANATOMY OF THE HUMAN LUNG. The Prize Essay to which the Fothergillian Gold Medal was awarded by the Medical Society of London. Post 8vo. cloth, 6s. 6d.
III.
RESEARCHES ON THE NATURE, PATHOLOGY, AND
TREATMENT OF EMPHYSEMA OF THE LUNGS, AND ITS RELATIONS WITH OTHER DISEASES OF THE CHEST. With Engravings. 8vo. cloth, 5s.

ALLAN WEBB, M.D., F.R.C.S.L.
THE SURGEON'S READY RULES FOR OPERATIONS IN SURGERY. Royal 8vo. cloth, 10s. 6d.

J. SOELBERG WELLS.

I.
A TREATISE ON THE DISEASES OF THE EYE. With Coloured Plates and Wood Engravings. 8vo. cloth, 24s.

II.
ON LONG, SHORT, AND WEAK SIGHT, and their Treatment by the Scientific Use of Spectacles. Third Edition. With Plates. 8vo. cloth, 6s.

T. SPENCER WELLS, F.R.C.S.
SCALE OF MEDICINES FOR MERCHANT VESSELS. With Observations on the Means of Preserving the Health of Seamen, &c. &c. Seventh Thousand. Fcap. 8vo. cloth, 3s. 6d.

CHARLES WEST, M.D., F.R.C.P.
LECTURES ON THE DISEASES OF WOMEN. Third Edition. 8vo. cloth, 16s.

J. A. WHEELER.
HAND-BOOK OF ANATOMY FOR STUDENTS OF THE FINE ARTS. With Engravings on Wood. Fcap. 8vo., 2s. 6d.

JAMES WHITEHEAD, M.D., M.R.C.P.
ON THE TRANSMISSION FROM PARENT TO OFFSPRING OF SOME FORMS OF DISEASE, AND OF MORBID TAINTS AND TENDENCIES. Second Edition. 8vo. cloth, 10s. 6d.

C. J. B. WILLIAMS, M.D., F.R.C.P., F.R.S.
PRINCIPLES OF MEDICINE: An Elementary View of the Causes, Nature, Treatment, Diagnosis, and Prognosis, of Disease. With brief Remarks on Hygienics, or the Preservation of Health. The Third Edition. 8vo. cloth, 15s.

FORBES WINSLOW, M.D., D.C.L.OXON.
OBSCURE DISEASES OF THE BRAIN AND MIND. Fourth Edition. Carefully Revised. Post 8vo. cloth, 10s. 6d.

T. A. WISE, M.D., F.R.C.P.EDIN.
REVIEW OF THE HISTORY OF MEDICINE AMONG ASIATIC NATIONS. Two Vols. 8vo. cloth, 16s.

ERASMUS WILSON, F.R.C.S., F.R.S.

I.

THE ANATOMIST'S VADE-MECUM: A SYSTEM OF HUMAN
ANATOMY. With numerous Illustrations on Wood. Eighth Edition. Foolscap 8vo. cloth, 12s. 6d.

II.

ON DISEASES OF THE SKIN: A SYSTEM OF CUTANEOUS
MEDICINE. Sixth Edition. 8vo. cloth, 18s.

The same Work; illustrated with finely executed Engravings on Steel, accurately coloured. 8vo. cloth, 36s.

III.

HEALTHY SKIN: A Treatise on the Management of the Skin and Hair
in relation to Health. Seventh Edition. Foolscap 8vo. 2s. 6d.

IV.

PORTRAITS OF DISEASES OF THE SKIN. Folio. Fasciculi I.
to XII., completing the Work. 20s. each. The Entire Work, half morocco, £13.

V.

THE STUDENT'S BOOK OF CUTANEOUS MEDICINE AND
DISEASES OF THE SKIN. Post 8vo. cloth, 8s. 6d.

VI.

LECTURES ON EKZEMA AND EKZEMATOUS AFFEC-
TIONS; with an Introduction on the General Pathology of the Skin, and an Appendix of Essays and Cases. 8vo. cloth, 10s. 6d.

VII.

ON SYPHILIS, CONSTITUTIONAL AND HEREDITARY;
AND ON SYPHILITIC ERUPTIONS. With Four Coloured Plates. 8vo. cloth, 16s.

VIII.

A THREE WEEKS' SCAMPER THROUGH THE SPAS OF
GERMANY AND BELGIUM, with an Appendix on the Nature and Uses of Mineral Waters. Post 8vo. cloth, 6s. 6d.

IX.

THE EASTERN OR TURKISH BATH: its History, Revival in
Britain, and Application to the Purposes of Health. Foolscap 8vo., 2s.

G. C. WITTSTEIN.

PRACTICAL PHARMACEUTICAL CHEMISTRY: An Explanation
of Chemical and Pharmaceutical Processes, with the Methods of Testing the Purity of the Preparations, deduced from Original Experiments. Translated from the Second German Edition, by Stephen Darby. 18mo. cloth, 6s.

HENRY G. WRIGHT, M.D., M.R.C.P.

I.

UTERINE DISORDERS: their Constitutional Influence and Treatment.
8vo. cloth, 7s. 6d.

II.

HEADACHES; their Causes and their Cure. Fourth Edition. Fcap. 8vo.
2s. 6d.

CHURCHILL'S SERIES OF MANUALS.

Fcap. 8vo. cloth, 12s. 6d. each.

"We here give Mr. Churchill public thanks for the positive benefit conferred on the Medical Profession, by the series of beautiful and cheap Manuals which bear his imprint."— *British and Foreign Medical Review.*

AGGREGATE SALE, 154,000 COPIES.

ANATOMY. With numerous Engravings. Eighth Edition. By ERASMUS WILSON, F.R.C.S., F.R.S.

BOTANY. With numerous Engravings. By ROBERT BENTLEY, F.L.S., Professor of Botany, King's College. and to the Pharmaceutical Society.

CHEMISTRY. With numerous Engravings. Tenth Edition, 14s. By GEORGE FOWNES. F.R.S., H. BENCE JONES, M.D., F.R.S., and HENRY WATTS, B.A., F.R.S.

DENTAL SURGERY. With numerous Engravings. By JOHN TOMES, F.R.S.

EYE, DISEASES OF. With coloured Plates and Engravings on Wood. By C. MACNAMARA.

MATERIA MEDICA. With numerous Engravings. Fifth Edition. By J. FORBES ROYLE, M.D., F.R.S., and F. W. HEADLAND, M.D., F.R.C.P.

MEDICAL JURISPRUDENCE. With numerous Engravings. Eighth Edition. By ALFRED SWAINE TAYLOR, M.D., F.R.S.

PRACTICE OF MEDICINE. Second Edition. By G. HILARO BARLOW, M.D., M.A.

The MICROSCOPE and its REVELATIONS. With numerous Plates and Engravings. Fourth Edition. By W. B. CARPENTER, M.D., F.R.S.

NATURAL PHILOSOPHY. With numerous Engravings. Sixth Edition. By CHARLES BROOKE, M.B., M.A., F.R.S. *Based on the Work of the late Dr. Golding Bird.*

OBSTETRICS. With numerous Engravings. By W. TYLER SMITH, M.D., F.R.C.P.

OPHTHALMIC MEDICINE and SURGERY. With coloured Plates and Engravings on Wood. Third Edition. By T. WHARTON JONES, F.R.C.S., F.R.S.

PATHOLOGICAL ANATOMY. With numerous Engravings. By C. HANDFIELD JONES, M.B., F.R.S., and E. H. SIEVEKING, M.D., F.R.C.P.

PHYSIOLOGY. With numerous Engravings. Fourth Edition. By WILLIAM B. CARPENTER, M.D., F.R.S.

POISONS. Second Edition. By ALFRED SWAINE TAYLOR, M.D., F.R.S.

PRACTICAL ANATOMY. With numerous Engravings. Second Edition. By CHRISTOPHER HEATH, F.R.C.S.

PRACTICAL SURGERY. With numerous Engravings. Fourth Edition. By Sir WILLIAM FERGUSSON, Bart., F.R.C.S., F.R.S.

THERAPEUTICS. Second Edition. By E. J. Waring, M.D., M.R.C.P.

www.ingramcontent.com/pod-product-compliance
Lightning Source LLC
Chambersburg PA
CBHW022130160426
43197CB00009B/1224